Red and Blue

A Fractured Democracy

Cover photo National Museum of American
History

Star Spangled Banner

Table of Contents

Red and Blue

Blue

A Fractured Democracy

Revised 2024

For questions or feedback on this book, contact Mark at
Mdennis99@yahoo.com

Originally written in April 2016, this book has been updated in June 2024 with ChatGPT to improve grammar and flow, incorporate new relevant information, and modernize its content.

Introduction

The terms "Conservative" and "Liberal" are commonly used to define social, economic, or political opinions and relationships. These two terms mean different things in different settings and vary across different parts of the world and periods in history. Today, in the United States, the United Kingdom, and many other democracies, there is a clear divide between Conservatives and Liberals, more evident than ever before in history. This division between the Right and the Left, the Red and the Blue, has become so pronounced that it threatens to fracture democracy.

Political discourse in these countries has become impoverished, with few people getting along. Frustration, animosity, and anger are evident in many government inquiries, debates, and voting sessions, provoking a tug-of-war in which no one wins. Hostility toward other political parties has become ingrained in politicians' minds and the minds of the people. This was exemplified when, during one of President Obama's State of the Union speeches, a member of the other party yelled, "Liar!" This anger is largely due to a "witch's brew" of politicians bashing each other through negative campaigning and biased news sources. Every election year, it seems to worsen, almost to the point of boiling over.

More recently, this polarization was starkly exemplified after the 2020 election when Donald Trump claimed widespread election fraud, despite numerous recounts and court cases upholding the election's integrity. Trump's assertions of a "stolen election" not only fueled mistrust and animosity between political factions but also led to significant unrest, for Liberals, culminating in the January 6, 2021, "attack on the U.S. Capitol". This event underscored the dangerous consequences of entrenched partisan hostility and the urgent need for restoring trust in democratic processes and institutions. Many Conservatives felt their concerns were dismissed without proper investigation.

In his book "The Righteous Mind," Jonathan Haidt studies Conservative and Liberal psychology and cites interesting findings about both groups. He opens with the 1992 Los Angeles riots, where Rodney King, after being beaten by the Los Angeles police, shouted in frustration, "*Please, we can get along here, we all can get along*!"

But can we? Can we understand each other's differences and respectfully allow these differences to coexist? It's not that easy. Conservatives and Liberals think completely differently. Both groups use "conceptual metaphors"—different ways of understanding or seeing a common issue based on what each considers common sense. To each, the other's positions often seem offensively immoral or irrational. One thing is clear: both religion and politics are manifestations of one's basic moral makeup. How someone expresses themselves in these areas shows whether they are Conservative or Liberal.

Introduction

Conservatives typically approach most things through principles, self-discipline, and responsibility, which require strict obedience to standards, rules and laws. Moral strength is vital to them to stand against external and internal evils within oneself, family, or nation; to them, there is a clear distinction between right and wrong.

Conservatives love using metaphors in speech, talking about "darkness and light," being "in the shadows," or "on common ground," and often scold Liberals for not understanding their language. Most issues are seen by Conservatives as either good or bad, with punitive action to correct wrongdoing and rewards for good deeds. Morality and virtue are central to the Conservative political agenda, rooted in nationalism and the sovereignty, rights, and liberties of the people. They focus on the traditional family, nationalism, social stability, and support legislation to limit immigration and punish crime. They also believe in a free-market system and that the government should not regulate business or manage the economy but let the economy manage itself. Conservative values are often rooted in religious faith, and many Conservatives seek to apply these religious values to national laws and regulations, to the dismay of Liberals.

Liberals typically approach most things through social causes that address the needs of people, animals, and the environment. To them, this process encourages giving, cooperation, and training, producing an environment conducive to social productivity.

Liberalism derives from what some call the "Enlightenment tradition," which uses literal, rational, and issue-oriented discourse, at least in their minds. Morality to Liberals involves nurturing, assuming compassion and empathy, which entails sacrifices; helping people in need is a moral responsibility of the government. Many Liberals feel that metaphors are only words and that the use of rhetoric veils the issues; they believe concepts and ideas should be literal and straightforward. Conservatives feel this type of thinking is weak and prevents constructive discourse, as metaphors are part of everyone's cognitive understanding process.

To Liberals, the Conservative traditional and religious moral approach is suitable for mono-ethnic societies with common religious values. However, globalization has led to increased diversity in many countries. Major cities worldwide have become melting pots of various ethnic and religious traditions, rendering a single Conservative traditional and moral approach ineffective socially or politically. This new diverse environment encourages the evolution of non-traditional families, including mixed-race, mixed-religion families, and same-sex marriages with children from previous marriages or adopted children.

In his book "*Moral Politics*," George Lakoff explains that these two political and social opinions can be seen figuratively as two different family models or moral systems: the "strict fatherly discipline" approach and the "nurturing mother" approach. Most people do not consciously think about what they say in everyday conversations; words come from deeply held beliefs, often aligned with one of these two models. Cognitive processes largely align with either approach, influenced by genetics, family, friends, and life experiences.

This reasoning process is also heavily influenced by religion and culture, shaping what is deemed acceptable or not and establishing social norms. Whether one is Liberal or Conservative, this thinking process that evolves over a lifetime directly influences one's conceptual metaphors. These metaphors are perceptions produced in the mind when concepts and ideas arise, a never-ending process.

The differences between the right and left, Conservative and Liberal, lie in how each person cognitively conceptualizes or associates various issues. A conceptual metaphor is a figurative comparison, a way of intellectualizing or reasoning through an issue. A Conservative may view education from a "strict fatherly" business perspective, seeing it as an "investment" requiring strict self-discipline. In contrast, a Liberal might see it from a "nurturing mother" perspective, emphasizing the need to "grow" and "become stronger" through proper mental "nourishment." National political policies are often derived from this family-based morality, constructed from unconscious metaphors in legislators' minds.

Lakoff explores the metaphors used in government and politics, illustrating how these metaphors visualize the nation as a family. He shows the differences between Conservative and Liberal political positions, known as progressives, and how both operate with different views of family maintenance. Both approaches induce moral priorities into society in different ways.

Core to Conservative politics are morality and family. The family-based "strict father" approach emphasizes self-control, self-discipline, respect for authority, for rules and standards. For Conservatives, moral self-interest improves the overall self-interests of everyone. Through personal responsibility and discipline, big government becomes unnecessary, as the marketplace will regulate itself. Conservatives believe the government's role is to protect individual liberty and traditional values with a strong national defense system. Thus, Conservative policies generally emphasize individual empowerment to solve personal problems.

Liberal politics also centers on family-based morality, approaching issues from a "nurturing mother" perspective. This perspective emphasizes the importance of empathy and understanding, advocating for extending a helping hand to those in need. Moral nurturance requires not only taking care of oneself first to be able to help others effectively but also creating a supportive and caring community. According to Abraham Maslow's Hierarchy of Needs, self-esteem and self-actualization—the desire for self-fulfillment—are crucial elements for individuals to thrive. Liberals believe that the government has a moral responsibility to ensure that all citizens have access to essential services, including healthcare, education, and support for the needy, such as those with disabilities, the poor, and the elderly. By doing so, they argue, society as a whole becomes more compassionate, equitable, and just, ultimately benefiting everyone.

According to Jonathan Haidt's research, morality for Conservatives includes loyalty, respect for authority, and sacredness, values not as highly regarded by most Liberals. Many Liberals take offense to this approach, as their perspectives on family and authority often differ from traditional views. Morality for Liberals includes compassion, mercy, and understanding, values not as highly valued by Conservatives, who may find compulsory giving objectionable and forgiveness as weak. Conservatives argue that morality is often relegated to religious organizations due to the separation of church and state, while for them, morality is based on religious faith and principles, focusing on the family.

Approximately 40% of the electorate in the United States consistently adheres to "strict" politics, while another 40% is "nurturing" in its politics. Only about 20% are middle-of-the-road, a division seen worldwide, especially in educated, first-world countries. This complexity arises as most people are Conservative in some areas and Liberal in others. Family life may lean in one direction, while politics may lean in another. Idealistic Conservatives and Liberals tend not to compromise, while pragmatic individuals can work together.

Right and Left, Red and Blue, Conservative or Liberal, are often viewed as a spectrum from one extreme to another. In reality, most people hold varying opinions and lean both ways depending on the issue. For example, some may be fiscally Conservative but Liberal on environmental issues. No one is truly a "Moderate" politically; they tend to be Conservative or progressive, idealistic or pragmatic, depending on the issue. People who claim to be completely moderate often appear apathetic and unconcerned with issues.

The term "right-wing" has historically applied to Conservatives supportive of traditional political and religious institutions. The term "left-wing" was associated with unorthodox political or religious perspectives. Today, people on the right believe society is better off with minimal government intervention, while those on the left support a larger governmental role, which generally requires higher taxes.

These views vary by gender and geography; men tend to lean right, while women lean left. In the United States, those living in the South or Midwest tend to be more Conservative compared to those in the Northeast or West Coast, who are more Liberal. Racial differences also play a role, with minorities like Blacks and Hispanics leaning left, while whites lean right, often influenced by wealth disparities.

Liberals naturally see it as common sense for the government to help people in need and assist with social programs. Likewise, it is common sense for Conservatives to view the government as requiring citizens to be disciplined and self-reliant. It is the pragmatic and realistic individuals, whether Conservative or Liberal, who refuse to let ideology supersede sensibility and get things done. It is the idealists and extremists on the Left and Right, who will not allow practicality to override their moral principles, that have produced the quagmire we are now in, refusing to budge in their stances based on principle—an endless tug-of-war.

In the late 1800s and early 1900s, Republicans tended to be more liberal on social policy, while Democrats were considered the leading social conservatives who held on to traditional family values. The Republican Party in the North originally materialized in an attempt to abolish slavery, with Abraham Lincoln as the symbol of the party during this period. When Johnson signed the Civil Rights Act of 1964, the Democratic South began to move over to the Republican Party mainly because Johnson was a Democrat. Moderate Democrats lost ground in the South during the 1980s and 1990s, and today the South is primarily Republican.

One cannot simply infer that Republicans are always right and Democrats are always left, as things change over time. People vary on different issues depending on whether they are male or female, black, brown, or white, and gay or straight, even though they may lean Conservative or Liberal on primary issues; nothing is absolute.

Today, cultural matters related to sex and marriage, have the greatest divisiveness in the nation when it comes to morality. These issues include gay and lesbian relationships, having a child out of wedlock, having sex before marriage, being divorced, or being in mixed-race and mixed-religion couples. Liberals overwhelmingly accept these as non-moral issues of personal freedom, while over half of the Conservatives researched consider these morally unacceptable. The underlying basis for Conservatives is that this way of life does not benefit or strengthen the family or the nation and, in fact, undermines their cultural and religious traditions and values.

Issues related to life also causes major conflict, such as abortion, research using embryonic stem cells, euthanasia, the death penalty, and military involvement. These issues can be confusing, as Liberals tend to support abortion, embryonic stem cell research, and euthanasia while opposing war and the death penalty. Conservatives support the death penalty and military activity while opposing abortion, embryonic stem cell research, and euthanasia.

Both Conservatism and Liberalism have strong opinions and reasons for their beliefs. Both prosper in their own way because they align with how people in their respective groups already think and feel. Neither ideology truly persuades people one way or the other through reason; they simply appeal to sentiments that people already hold.

Introduction

People's minds do not change due to reason; one gains approval as a Conservative or a Liberal by appealing to the moral instinct that is already built in genetically, environmentally, and socially over a lifetime. Trying to appeal to reason generally gets nowhere fast, as people's minds tend to be already made up; only changes to one's social environment over time can do this. Intuition drives humanity, with reason coming in second. How one perceives they are viewed by others is much more important than what one perceives as reasonable or rational.

The primary issues that fracture our nation are abortion, affirmative action, animal rights, capital punishment, constitutional interpretation, crime, drugs, economics, education, energy, and the environment. They also include euthanasia, government spending, gun control, healthcare, human rights, immigration, individual liberty and privacy, the military and war, prayer in school, race, sex, taxes, and wealth. We will review all of these aspects in the following chapters from both Liberal and Conservative positions.

Red and Blue II

The Right

Conservatism tends to want to keep traditions as they are and not allow them to change if possible. No matter where Conservatives are in the world, they strive to hold on to the culture and traditional values passed down through their families from generation to generation. The origins of Conservative thought date back to ancient Greek Athenian Democracy in the 5th century BC and Roman self-government as a Republic.

The foundation of modern Conservatism began to flourish in England as far back as 1215 with the Magna Carta, where even King John declared himself subject to the laws of the land. These rights set forth in the Magna Carta eventually became the heart of the American Revolution and the source of the American Constitution and the Bill of Rights. The Magna Carta still endures as an important symbol of liberty.

The primary principles of Conservative thought include limited government and providing liberty (Buckley, pg. 41). This liberty means the freedom to pursue one's goals in a free competitive market system, emphasizing individual empowerment to solve personal problems. Individual liberty, personal responsibility, traditional values, and a strong national defense are vital; a strong military ensures peace, and liberty preserves happiness. People must be responsible for themselves and their families, and the government must be prevented from intruding on the daily lives of the people (Garry, pg. 2).

1

Everyone benefits from lowering taxes; when the most vibrant and prosperous members of society thrive, they create jobs and affluence. Political leaders must help reduce bureaucratic interference to allow people to pursue their goals, improving the standard of living for everyone. Even President John F. Kennedy, a Liberal Democrat, understood this principle, saying in 1962, "The purpose of cutting taxes now is not to incur a budget deficit, but to achieve the more prosperous, expanding economy which can bring a budget surplus" (Hayward, pg. 77).

Family, heritage, tradition, and country are deeply rooted in Conservative principles (Lakoff, 2010, pg. 30). Protecting the family, heritage, and country from harm often discourages nontraditional ways of life and thinking. The Conservative stance on abortion, drugs, capital punishment, crime, and gun control reflects their commitment to family health. Their views on human and animal rights, immigration, race, and religion are influenced by their perspectives on tradition and heritage, while their views on liberty, the military, and war are shaped by their nationalism. Conservative opinions on economics, prosperity, wealth, government spending, and taxes also stem from their family values and love for their country.

There are several groups of Conservatives. Fiscal Conservatives, including Libertarians, are concerned with careful government spending and the health of the economy (Zelizer, pg. 148). They believe it is not the government's responsibility to control poverty, education, or public health but that of the state, local community, and church. They oppose Affirmative Action, which encourages government spending on improving equality in education, race, and sexual preference.

Religious Conservatives, such as the Moral Majority, The Family Research Council, and Focus on the Family, promote political engagement and the expansion of religion into social life (Green, pg. 158). They seek to integrate religious principles into laws that maintain traditional family and social values, addressing issues like abortion, homosexuality, sexual promiscuity, and prostitution.

Social Conservatives are primarily concerned with continuing their heritage and are often very nationalistic, valuing loyalty, sanctity, and authority (Haidt, 2013, pg. 368). They oppose changes to traditional ways of thinking, especially when such changes are perceived as threats to Conservative values. Issues like drug use, abortion, prostitution, euthanasia, and same-sex marriage are seen as direct challenges to family values, causing conflict and breaking up families.

Stereotypes of Conservatism include labels like pro-business, personal responsibility, pro-life, pro-gun, fundamentalist Christian, pro-school prayer, Southern, NASCAR fan, wealthy, creationist, and sports fan. Negative stereotypes include terms like racist, warmonger, pro-censorship, white male, redneck, cowboy, isolationist, greedy, and intolerant. While these stereotypes often oversimplify various perspectives within the Conservative movement, they contain some truth.

Morality is at the heart of Conservative doctrine, focusing directly on the family. Understanding right and wrong, justice, discipline, strength, courage, and self-reliance are the foundations of their beliefs and traditions (Russel, pg. 336).

Abortion

Conservatives overwhelmingly oppose abortion, viewing it as the murder of a human being. More than 80 percent of Conservatives polled believe that human life begins at conception and that unborn children have the same rights as any other human being (Alcorn, pg. 51). Exceptions to their anti-abortion stance are rare, often only considered when the mother's life is in danger, and even then, some Conservatives find it unacceptable. They argue that if someone cannot financially or emotionally raise a child, the child should be put up for adoption. For Conservatives, "unborn children have a protectable interest in life, health, and well-being" (Goldstein, pg. 37).

Since the Roe vs. Wade Supreme Court decision in 1973, which ruled that prohibiting abortion was unconstitutional, Conservatives have strongly opposed taxpayer-funded abortions. They support legislation that prohibits partial-birth and late-term abortions. To Conservatives, the Liberal organization Planned Parenthood is seen as dedicated to the prevention of parenthood, using taxpayer dollars to help women have abortions. Conservatives push to vote for politicians who promise to stop taxpayer funding of Planned Parenthood (Engs, pg. 234). They believe that the millions of abortions performed in the United States have eroded their civil culture more than any other issue.

Liberals find it irrational that anti-abortion activists support capital punishment. They question how Conservatives can advocate for the right to life while supporting the death penalty and military actions that result in the loss of lives, including fathers and brothers. Liberals argue that the emotional and economic devastation caused by the death of a husband and father in war is more significant than that of a two-month-old fetus.

Affirmative Action

Affirmative Action has its roots in the 1964 Civil Rights Act, which outlawed discrimination based on race, color, religion, or sex. It aimed to provide opportunities in education and employment for those who had been discriminated against. Conservative opposition to Affirmative Action emerged in the 1970s when some whites were excluded from specific educational benefits given to minorities. This led to perceptions of reverse discrimination, where minorities with lower test scores, for example, were admitted to universities over more qualified white applicants (Carlisle, pg. 8).

By the 1980s, most Conservatives believed that Affirmative Action was no longer necessary. They argued that it had served its purpose and that continuing it was unfair to those who did not receive the same benefits. Some Conservatives felt there was a time and place for Affirmative Action, but the majority believed it had outlived its usefulness and was now promoting inequality rather than addressing it.

Animal Rights

Conservatives generally love wild game hunting and oppose legislation that restricts hunting and gun ownership. Similarly, in the farming industry, the mass production of beef, veal, milk, pork, and chicken has thrived with Conservative support and government assistance. Conservatives aim to limit regulations concerning what Liberals regard as animal abuse and to legislate funding to support the livestock industry. Historically, Conservative traditions have reinforced a utilitarian view of animals, seeing them as lesser beings created for human needs, such as food and property (Regan, pg. 143).

Liberals often criticize Conservatives for lacking compassion toward animal rights, a perspective that may be tied to Biblical teachings that emphasize man's dominion over animals. Consequently, many Conservatives have no issues with animal testing for medical studies or the mass production of animals for food and clothing if done humanely.

Statistics show that feelings toward animal rights are relatively balanced, though organizations like PETA (People for the Ethical Treatment of Animals) would disagree. Regarding wearing clothing made from animal fur, 54% of Democrats and 67% of Republicans support it. For cloning animals, 34% of Democrats are opposed compared to 27% of Republicans. Regarding medical product testing on animals, 58% of Democrats and 62% of Republicans are in favor (Dautrich, pg. 361). However, a clear difference exists between Conservatives and Liberals when it comes to owning pets. Conservatives prefer dogs that are loyal and obedient, while Liberals prefer empathetic and non-submissive dogs (Haidt, 2013, pg. 188).

In terms of animal farms, Conservatives prioritize business efficiency over animal rights, arguing that human compassion toward animals is an obligation, not an entitlement. They believe in respecting all life as God's creation while acknowledging that animals are provided to humans for food and clothing. Conservatives often criticize PETA's extreme actions, such as throwing red paint on fur wearers and comparing animal farm conditions to Nazi concentration camps. They find these actions excessive and view PETA's stance, including opposition to fishing, as extreme (Farmer, pg. 119).

Capital Punishment

Most Conservatives support capital punishment and the death penalty, often basing their stance on religious principles (Farmer, pg. 118). They believe capital punishment suits the crime of murder and is neither cruel nor unusual. Despite DNA evidence and scientific findings proving the innocence of some death row inmates and highlighting racial profiling issues, Conservatives maintain that capital punishment is necessary. They argue that lessons learned will reduce risks going forward and believe strict regulations and appropriate punishment are essential to deter crime.

Liberals see it as contradictory for Conservatives to support both capital punishment and the pro-life, anti-abortion stance. They question why a grown man with family and children should be valued less than an unborn fetus.

Constitution Interpretation

"Originalists," such as Justice Antonin Scalia and Justice Clarence Thomas, interpret the Constitution based on the original intent of its writers. This approach, known as strict constructionism, implies that no discretion is acceptable for Supreme Court judges. Originalists believe that the Constitution should be amended through serious public debate and that its interpretation should be uniform with the original text's meaning at the time of its acceptance.

Supporters of originalism argue that this approach prevents judicial activism, where judges might impose their personal views on the law rather than adhering to the Constitution. They assert that the Constitution is a stable, enduring document whose meaning should not fluctuate with changing social or political trends. This stability, they argue, provides a clear, predictable framework for governance and protects against arbitrary shifts in legal interpretations. Originalists maintain that any necessary changes to the Constitution should be made through the amendment process, ensuring that such changes reflect the will of the people and not the preferences of a few judges. Critics, however, argue that this approach can be overly rigid, potentially ignoring the evolving nature of society and the need for the law to adapt to contemporary issues. Nonetheless, originalists hold that their method ensures fidelity to the democratic principles upon which the Constitution was founded.

Crime

Conservatives believe that humans naturally know right from wrong through "Natural Law" and that proper punishment is the solution to violent crime. They adhere to the ancient concept of "an eye for an eye" from Hammurabi's Code. Conservatives argue that treating people as they treat others is a moral imperative (Nathanson, pg. 73).

Liberals are viewed by Conservatives as being soft on crime, often blaming societal factors rather than individual responsibility. Conservatives oppose early prison releases to reduce costs, seeing it as dangerous. They believe committing a crime is a rational choice made by those who think they can get away with it. To prevent crime, they argue for increasing the odds of getting caught and intensifying punishment severity.

The primary function of government, according to Conservatives, is to preserve the security and safety of its people against enemies, both foreign and domestic. They argue that criminal behavior cannot be eradicated but can be challenged through a moral society where reward and punishment are paramount (Lakoff, pg. 209).

Conservatives contend that crime causes poverty, not the other way around. They argue that dropping out of school leads to crime and that illegal activities like drug sales undermine productivity. Conservatives believe young men who are idle and lack jobs contribute to crime rates.

Drugs

Most Conservatives believe that recreational drugs, deemed illegal by the government, should be punished accordingly. Legal prescription drugs must be regulated and controlled to prevent abuse, especially among adolescents. However, this regulation should be at the state level, not the federal level, as they believe the federal government has too much control over people's lives.

Libertarian-leaning Conservatives argue that individuals should manage their own health without government interference (Lakoff, pg. 294). They believe people should be free to do what they want unless it harms others, including drug, tobacco, and alcohol use.

The Right

Fiscal Conservatives have historically supported legislation subsidizing tobacco farmers and alcohol corporations, indicating that personal health is not their primary concern. However, they support the military and prison systems for moral values and business profitability. Prisons, filled with drug offenders, represent financial interest for Conservatives.

Religious Conservatives oppose tobacco, alcohol, and drug use for personal health reasons, viewing the body as a temple. They argue that widespread use of these substances harms personal and national health. They associate Liberal attitudes toward drugs and alcohol with decreased religious commitment and lack of self-control (Chamberlain, pg. 193).

Drug money finances gangs and crime within the United States and foreign cartels, making it a moral issue for religious Conservatives. Both Conservatives and Liberals have supported the War on Drugs, except for recreational drugs like marijuana, which many Liberals want legalized. Conservatives see marijuana legalization as a threat to patriotism and national security (Bertram, pg. 98), believing it leads to worse drugs.

Conservatives criticize Liberals for prioritizing "safety, fairness, equality, sobriety, health, pets, and other people's children" over liberty and free will (Harsanyi, pg. 3). Liberals see a contradiction in Conservatives' rejection of government regulations on personal choices while supporting regulation of recreational drugs. Conservatives argue that illegal drugs, like prostitution, are offensive and immoral enough to warrant government intervention (Harsanyi, pg. 13).

Economics

Conservatives believe that the government needs to tax people and businesses less and spend less money. However, this belief depends on what is to be cut; cutting government spending to balance the budget should be the priority. Conservatives prefer to cut social programs rather than military budgets. To Liberals, these Conservatives would sacrifice anything the government can offer just to keep taxes low for the wealthy, poisoning social trust (Haidt, 2013, pg. 445).

For Conservatives, higher income earners should have an incentive to grow businesses and make more money. Taxing the wealthy discourages profitability and always trickles down to the workers and the marketplace in lost jobs. Charity is the responsibility of the people and not of corporations and businesses. A business is there to be profitable and grow, and most Conservatives believe that these businesses in the private sector can provide most services more efficiently than the government can through competition (Lakoff, 2010, pg. 328). The government does not have the right to spend large amounts of money and then expect the taxpayers to pay for it.

Fiscal Conservatives believe that over time, deep tax cuts across the board will eventually pay for themselves through economic growth. They argue that the government has taken tax money unfairly from hardworking, sensible people to support irresponsible fools (Haidt, 2013, pg. 181). This undermines fairness and economic profitability as taking money away from those who make money prevents them from providing more jobs.

Education and Children

Conservatives feel it is not the Federal Government's responsibility to manage children's education issues, as this is traditionally the concern of the community and families. If anything, it is the responsibility of the local and State government to ensure that the safety and education of children are managed properly. Most Conservatives feel that the Federal Government needs to get out of the education business altogether, and eliminating the Department of Education is one of their priorities (Lakoff, 2010, pg. 229). Most, if they could, would rather take their children out of the public school system and send them to religious or military schools that they feel are better equipped to teach strict moral teachings to their children. To them, having a school voucher system would create competition and encourage the public school system to perform better. These vouchers could give more parents the ability to choose better schools for their children that today only the wealthy can afford (Farmer, pg. 82). This improved competition would shut down the public schools that cannot compete with the private schools and Charter Schools and therefore improve the education of all American children.

Conservatives support Charter Schools that receive public funding but are run independently of the public school system. Many of these schools are partially funded with grants from corporations and operate without the influence of teachers' unions. Many Conservatives believe in shutting down the old school system and building up a "reconstituted" school system. This would be accomplished by expanding privately-run, non-union Charter Schools that would theoretically improve the education system dramatically, bringing America back to prosperity. These Charter Schools are supported by the same Conservative religious and political groups that support the school voucher program, including business entities such as the Chamber of Commerce (Wilson, pg. 352).

For those without the luxury of Charter Schools, the only other opportunity to keep their kids out of the Liberal school system was to homeschool. By 2004, about one out of every 25 children in the United States was homeschooled, with most States requiring some sort of educational evaluation to ensure the kids are learning (Carlisle, pg. 621).

Energy

Most Conservatives are pro-energy and focus on American independence from foreign oil with increased drilling for oil, gas, and mining for coal domestically (Lakoff, 2010, pg. 408). Concern over greenhouse gases and global warming is seen as a lot of hype by many Conservatives, as scientists have been able to spin things both ways. The deregulation of the energy industry and even the elimination of the Department of Energy are desires for many Conservatives as well. Government regulations incur great costs for the energy business and create a lot of organizational difficulties. Ronald Reagan, during his presidential campaign in 1980, even promised to abolish the Department of Energy (Margulies, pg. 27).

These regulations for environmental protection and wildlife protection have clearly tied the energy industry's hands and have also dramatically increased their costs. Government regulations on the industry hinder capitalism and the free market economy and stifle job growth. With oil costs as low as they are now, the energy industry just can't compete with government-subsidized companies in the Middle East who do not have such rules or concerns. Many oil fields in the American Midwest are being shut down because they are not worth keeping open. With oil down from $100 a barrel in 2014 to about $43 a barrel in 2015, many in the energy business are calling it quits and selling off their equipment at auction.

Ethanol made from government-subsidized grain grown by farmers in the Midwest also decreases demand for oil and drives oil prices down. Many Conservatives blame the EPA, Democrats, and left-leaning Republicans for this negative effect on their business and look at these subsidies as corporate welfare. The primary reasoning behind the ethanol subsidies is that it is both "greener" as a renewable fuel and a way to wean America from dependency on

Middle Eastern oil. In a way, it is great for the farmer but it costs the American taxpayer billions a year and undermines a free-market society (Lakoff, 2010, pg. 168). Many strong Conservatives feel that biofuel is already over-subsidized by the Federal Government and argue that no tax money should be used to fund biofuels.

Environment

Conservatives generally do not believe that Global Warming is a threat to our civilization. They view this concept as being mainly driven by Liberals who are overly concerned for natural habitats at the expense of business and taxpayer dollars. For example, the petroleum industry is particularly affected by regulations on offshore oil production and oil pipeline restrictions, which increase oil costs and reduce supplies; environmental regulations get in the way of profitability (Lakoff, 2010, pg. 409). Conservatives would rather prioritize the needs of businesses and the industry community than invest in environmental programs, which they believe, is based on what they consider to be "hocus pocus" policies driven by sentiment. They argue that countries like Saudi Arabia, China, and Mexico do not have these extra costs, making it hard to compete equitably.

Many Conservatives believe that scientific studies show humanity has not necessarily caused the changes seen in the Earth's temperature, viewing global temperature changes as a natural phenomenon supported by some scientists. They argue that environmental laws aimed at reducing greenhouse gases will only waste money without benefiting the environment, ultimately leading to increased energy prices, higher taxes, and job loss. In the early 2000s, the George W. Bush administration claimed that the EPA did not have the authority to control greenhouse gases and that it was unwise to do so (Wilson, pg. 222). The Supreme Court eventually overturned this decision in 2007. Although George Bush promised to regulate carbon dioxide in his 2000 White House campaign, he pulled the U.S. out of the Kyoto Accords a year later because the proposed regulations were deemed too costly for industry. He later described the proposal as "an unrealistic and ever-tightening straitjacket" on the American economy.

Euthanasia

Conservatives hold a strong moral conviction that neither euthanasia nor physician-assisted suicide should be lawful. They fear that these practices could eventually extend to non-terminal patients, including those with mental illnesses or depression who simply do not want to live (Forgas, pg. 66). They consider intentionally ending the life of anyone, even a terminally ill person, as immoral and unethical. They believe that easing suffering with compassionate care should be the focus for the terminally ill. Conservatives argue that legalizing euthanasia or physician-assisted suicide could lead to compulsory euthanasia, with people making judgments on behalf of others, essentially playing God by deciding when and who should die and how. This, they contend, would undermine the intrinsic value and sanctity of human life, setting a dangerous precedent for society. Additionally, they worry that it could erode trust between patients and healthcare providers.

"Passive Voluntary Euthanasia," where a patient asks not to be kept on life support and to naturally die, is legal in all states. Most Conservatives argue that "life has an intrinsic sanctity that must be respected and protected at all times" (Green, pg. 864). "Active Voluntary Euthanasia," where lethal medication is intentionally administered by the physician or someone else to induce death, is considered illegal even if requested by the patient and actioned by a physician. As of 2015, Active Voluntary Euthanasia is legal only in a few countries such as Belgium, Colombia, Ireland, and the Netherlands.

"Physician-Assisted Suicide," where the physician provides the means for an ill patient to take their own life, is legal in many countries and several states. The 400 BC Hippocratic Oath, which doctors still swear by today, states, "…Nor shall any man's plea cause me to administer poison to anyone; neither will I counsel any man to do so." In 2001, the Bush Administration tried to use the "Controlled Substances Act" to challenge the "Oregon Death with Dignity Act," but the Supreme Court ruled that the government could not enforce this act against physicians who prescribe these types of medications legally.

Most religions prohibit suicide and euthanasia, forming the founding principles for many Conservatives. The Roman Catholic Church's own "Declaration on Euthanasia" states that euthanasia and assisted suicide are "crimes against life."

Conservatives believe God is the creator of all life, and the innocent life of the unborn child or the critically ill cancer patient is only His to take. To cause death by assisted suicide or euthanasia is seen as murder and playing God. However, Liberals often take issue with this stance, pointing out that many who oppose assisted suicide or euthanasia support the death penalty and military actions around the world, which involve intentionally killing and playing God.

Government Spending

Conservatives continue to push back on government spending, emphasizing cuts to social and health programs as well as environmental protection. National defense, however, is never an option for cuts, as this would reduce the nation's ability to protect its interests worldwide (Lakoff, 2010, pg. 192). Too many Conservatives, national security is more important than education, welfare, or the nation's highway and infrastructure, especially in times when ISIS terrorists threaten to strike at the heart of the homeland.

Conservatives tend to be more "anti-federalist" and prefer a smaller Federal Government with less regulation and a more literal interpretation of the Constitution. They would rather have most social services funded at the state level and provided by the private sector in a free market, rather than managed by ineffective Federal Government wasting of taxpayer dollars (Green, pg. 261).

Gun Control

Gun control is highly contested by Conservatives in America, as the Second Amendment of the Constitution guarantees the right to bear arms. The majority of Conservatives are opposed to gun control, viewing it similarly to other federal regulations like those that control public education and the environment, which they believe only increase taxation on people and businesses (Lakoff, 2010, pg. 294). Conservatives believe that the Federal Government must be limited in its ability to restrict one's right to own weapons for self-protection and hunting; if anything, these controls should be issues assessed by individual states.

The right to bear arms is enshrined in the Second Amendment to the United States Constitution, which states:

A well-regulated militia, being necessary to the security of a free State, the right of the people to keep and bear arms, shall not be infringed.

In the landmark 2008 case of District of Columbia v. Heller, the Supreme Court ruled that this amendment also applies to an individual's right to self-defense in the home, not just the defense of a nation with a militia or military (Garry, pg. 57-58). This decision has been pivotal in shaping the contemporary Conservative stance on gun ownership, reinforcing the belief that individuals should have the autonomy to protect themselves without excessive government interference.

Healthcare

Conservatives politically prefer minimal government intervention and advocate limiting its role to protecting individual liberties and rights. They argue that healthcare should be provided through competitive private industry to maintain cost efficiency. Government-run healthcare, they contend, increases costs due to reduced competition and necessitates larger bureaucratic structures that hinder the free market process (Lakoff, 2010, pg. 168). Conservatives generally support deregulation of commerce and believe that government should not be involved in healthcare, favoring free market solutions over taxpayer-funded government programs (Farmer, pg. 102). A healthcare marketplace driven by consumer choice, they argue, would reduce costs more effectively than governmental regulation.

Human Rights

Conservatives view human rights issues predominantly through a domestic lens, often perceiving international human rights concerns as left-wing causes originating outside the United States. They tend to resist international programs and institutions, citing concerns over including countries lacking basic liberties and governed undemocratically (Haidt, 2013, pg. 204). Many Conservatives believe existing U.S. laws provide sufficient protection against human rights abuses domestically.

Conservatives prioritize rights such as the right to life (particularly concerning the fetus), the right to bear arms, property rights, and freedom from excessive government control (Lakoff, 2010, pg. 150). They argue that their conservative policies promote human rights by fostering economic growth and do not infringe on minority rights. Conservatives advocate for disciplined and restrained human rights programs that avoid careless aid distribution without stringent review and majority approval, criticizing what they see as liberal social engineering efforts under the guise of "human rights." They emphasize a philosophy of "natural rights" over broader human rights initiatives.

Conservatives often oppose what they view as irresponsible human rights movements such as feminism and LGBTQ+ activism, viewing them as threats to traditional family values and national cohesion. They advocate for addressing global human rights issues through private, non-governmental efforts rather than taxpayer-funded handouts, promoting a philosophy akin to "teach a man to fish" rather than perpetual dependency.

No one should receive special privileges based solely on their identity; Conservatives believe that merit should determine rewards. This philosophy prioritizes their community and nation over global concerns (Haidt, 2013, pg. 204). They advocate for focusing on domestic issues first and entrusting nonprofit social and religious groups with addressing human rights challenges abroad.

Conservatives often criticize liberal policies for redistributing wealth, viewing it as taking from the successful to give to those who they believe should be self-sufficient (Lakoff, 2010, pg. 181). They argue that existing laws in the United States already protect the rights of all races and minorities equally, emphasizing the importance of individual effort and hard work without relying on preferential treatment.

Many Conservatives oppose Affirmative Action, seeing it as unfair and unnecessary compensation for historical injustices that they believe they are not responsible for addressing today. They argue that unhindered free enterprise, supported by limited government intervention, offers equal opportunities for minorities such as women, blacks, and Hispanics who are willing to earn their success through education and hard work.

Immigration

Conservatives generally oppose amnesty for undocumented immigrants and advocate against any moratorium on deporting those who have entered or remained in the country illegally. Many view undocumented immigrants as "illegals" and "lawbreakers" who should face imprisonment or deportation (Lakoff, 2010, pg. 187). They support bolstering border enforcement with measures like enhanced physical barriers, increased surveillance using military personnel, and deploying armed UAVs and drones.

For most Conservatives, legal immigration through established processes, such as those outlined in the proposed Dream Act, is acceptable (Bush, pg. 12). The primary concern lies with illegal immigrants who circumvent these legal channels. The influx of undocumented workers willing to accept lower wages can displace well-paid Americans, driving down wages and fostering reliance on illegal labor.

Illegal immigration is also viewed as a national security issue, contributing to increased unemployment rates, violent crimes, drug trafficking, and gang activity (Lakoff, 2014, pg. 72). Conservatives express concern that many illegal immigrants do not share traditional American values, impacting societal norms and cultural integrity. The concept of "anchor babies," where children born to illegal immigrants on U.S. soil gain automatic citizenship, complicates efforts to repatriate their parents; this is due to federal sponsorship restrictions for minors. This legal principle stems from the interpretation of the 14th Amendment to the U.S. Constitution, which grants citizenship to anyone born on American soil, regardless of their parents' immigration status. As a result, children born to illegal immigrants, often referred to as anchor babies, become legal citizens, which can complicate efforts to enforce immigration laws and return their parents to their countries of origin.

Liberty, Privacy, and Property

Conservatives staunchly uphold liberty and the pursuit of happiness as foundational principles of the United States, particularly emphasizing the right to bear arms enshrined in the Second Amendment. However, when issues of personal liberty intersect with what they consider unethical behaviors, such as recreational drug use or unconventional sexual practices (Garry, pg. 53), many Conservatives support legislation to regulate these activities. They argue that historically, laws addressing such issues, like Prohibition in the 1920s, have been motivated by moral considerations and enacted despite public opposition.

Concerning personal privacy, Conservatives prioritize safeguarding against governmental intrusion into private communications, such as monitoring phone calls or internet activities, which they view as necessary only in the context of combating terrorism or during times of war. They assert that the federal government's role should primarily focus on preserving the fundamental freedoms and rights deeply rooted in the nation's history and traditions (Garry, pg. 52).

In terms of property rights, Conservatives adamantly defend the right to own and possess property, citing the protections outlined in the Fifth Amendment. They critique what they perceive as unjust property taxation, arguing that excessive taxes effectively diminish private ownership and unfairly burden individuals, undermining true economic freedom and autonomy.

Military and War

Conservatives love the military primarily because it defends America's way of life and protects its interests overseas. The military to them shows the clear difference between what is good and what is evil. A strong military can be used in a way to chastise and destroy America's enemies and those who threaten America through terrorist action; this is American Justice. Evil to them must be resisted, sometimes by violent means; freedom is worth fighting and dying for.

Downsizing the military would leave America in a more vulnerable position. Today many Conservatives believe that the United States is acting like a country in decline in how it deals with terrorists, ISIS, Syria and even Russia. It should be projecting military strength rather than set a line and then back off. Conservatives strongly believe that government programs must be limited and primarily delegated to the States. Federal Government programs involved with national defense and in crime prevention are some the few programs that Conservatives approve of (Buckley, pg. 92).

To the Conservatives, military veterans are seen as servants to the American people, offering even their lives for their freedom driven by hard work, self-discipline, and personal accountability. It is estimated that more than two-thirds of high ranking military officers consider themselves as Conservative (Bolt, pg. 350). Having a strong military coincides with the Conservatives sense of the countries power and strength as well as its history, heritage and traditions. To them the military should never be used for public services, the reconstruction of infrastructure or for supporting any political power. It is a powerful and dominant military that promotes peace; only with a strong military can we build a brighter future.

For Conservatives, it is through military power that freedom, peace, and prosperity are spread worldwide. They believe the Federal Government should primarily fund itself through taxes to ensure the safety, liberty, and freedom of its citizens (Buckley, pg. 92). The military's role, according to Conservatives, is to defend America's way of life and safeguard its political and financial interests both domestically and internationally.

Liberals find this perspective perplexing, given that the United States allocates approximately 40% of its tax revenues to the military—more than all other countries combined—a form of Conservative welfare, some argue. They question why this substantial budget isn't directed towards social programs benefiting the needy, such as support for the poor, sick, and elderly, rather than using taxpayer dollars to maintain global security forces.

Prayer in School

Conservatives advocate for promoting prayer in schools, believing it fosters positive values among children and helps prevent division. They believe that reintroducing prayer would restore moral guidance and reinforce the values upon which the nation was founded. Traditionally, these prayers have been rooted in Judeo-Christian faiths, but many now argue that in today's diverse society, allowing a moment of silence for all faiths to pray or meditate could be more inclusive than discouraging prayer altogether. Allowing voluntary prayer or moments of silence respects religious freedoms without endorsing any particular faith, fostering a sense of unity and respect for diverse beliefs among students. This approach, they argue, aligns with the spirit of religious liberty enshrined in the First Amendment, allowing individuals to freely exercise their faith in public settings without government interference.

The Supreme Court's 1962 decision in Engel vs. Vitale banned prayer from public schools, citing it as a violation of the Constitutional principle of separation of church and state; only Justice Potter Stewart dissented, arguing that the majority had "misapplied a great Constitutional principle" (Kommers, pg. 483).

In 1982, Ronald Reagan formally proposed an amendment to remove this legal obstacle to prayer in public schools, stating, "Restore the simple freedom of our citizens to offer prayer in public schools and institutions" (Brown, pg. 184).

This amendment proposed:

> *"Nothing in this Constitution shall be construed to prohibit individual or group prayer in public schools or other public institutions. No person shall be required by the United States or by any State to participate in prayer."*

The Right

Conservatives believe that local school districts are best positioned to address diversity issues and that the federal government should not impose restrictions on religious expression within these communities (Kommers, pg. 565). However, many moderate Conservatives opposed an amendment to reintroduce prayer in schools, fearing it could dilute religious practices to accommodate the varied beliefs across the United States.

Despite these debates, many Conservatives argue that while the First Amendment does not require amendment itself, there is a need to clarify its interpretation regarding religious expression in public settings. In the 1990s, Conservatives proposed the Religious Equality Amendment to the Constitution, which aimed to permit religious expression in public school forums (Carlisle, pg. 584). This amendment sought to reaffirm the rights of individuals to freely exercise their religious beliefs without government interference, aligning with the principles of religious liberty upheld by the Constitution.

Conservatives contend that allowing voluntary religious expression in schools fosters a respectful environment for diverse beliefs, promoting moral values and reinforcing the nation's heritage of religious freedom. They argue that such measures uphold individual liberties while respecting the separation of church and state, ensuring that public schools remain inclusive and accommodating to all faiths within their local communities.

This Amendment State:

> *"To secure the people's right to acknowledge God according to the dictates of conscience: The people's right to pray and to recognize their religious beliefs, heritage or traditions on public property, including schools, shall not be infringed.*
>
> *The government shall not require any person to join in prayer or other activity, initiate or designate school prayers, discriminate against religion, or deny equal access to a benefit on account of religion"* (Jurinski pg. 218).

The First Amendment to the Constitution States this:

> *"Congress shall make no law respecting an establishment of religion, or prohibiting the free exercise thereof; or abridging the freedom of speech, or of the press; or the right of the people peaceably to assemble, and to petition the Government for a redress of grievances"* (Jurinski, pg. 263).

To amend the Constitution, it requires the support of two-thirds of both the House and Senate, followed by ratification by three-fourths of the state legislatures—a process that has yet to occur. Liberals argue that such an amendment would grant local public school districts and administrators the authority to "evangelize" students with specific religious beliefs, primarily Protestant Christianity during regular school hours.

This, according to Liberals, would suggest that Conservatives oppose personal freedom, particularly freedom from religious influence (Kuru, pg. 42).

Liberals contend that allowing prayers or religious expressions in public schools, without clear guidelines protecting all religious and non-religious viewpoints equally, could lead to favoritism towards certain religious beliefs over others. They argue that public schools, as government institutions, should remain neutral in matters of religion to ensure that students of all backgrounds feel equally respected and included. This neutrality, they argue, upholds the First Amendment's principle of separating church and state, preventing any single religious viewpoint from dominating public educational spaces.

Conservatives, on the other hand, view such restrictions on religious expression in public schools as an infringement on their right to freely exercise their faith. They argue that allowing voluntary prayer or moments of silence for reflection in schools would promote moral values and foster a sense of community among students. Conservatives often point to historical traditions of prayer and religious observance in American public life as evidence that these practices are compatible with the nation's heritage and values.

The debate underscores deeper philosophical differences about the role of religion in public life and the extent to which government institutions should accommodate or restrict religious practices. Conservatives prioritize the preservation of religious traditions and values, seeing them as integral to American identity and social cohesion. Liberals, meanwhile, emphasize the importance of protecting individual rights and ensuring that public institutions remain inclusive and secular, free from any religious coercion or preference.

Racial Issues

Conservatives traditionally maintain close ties to their own ethnicity, particularly in terms of where they reside and whom they marry. They are more inclined than Liberals to emphasize group or tribal values, focusing on defending and fostering the growth of their ethnic community. Actions perceived as straining this protection or growth, such as pursuing personal educational or career opportunities outside the community, are often discouraged.

The imperative to protect the family or group naturally discourages behaviors deemed detrimental by the community, especially recreational sexual conduct without intentions of contributing to the community's growth; "Morality is Wholeness" (Lakoff, 2010, pg. 91). This protective stance extends to religious values, often manifesting as reluctance towards integrating with other religions and races, regardless of their geographic location—a perspective that may appear prejudiced to outsiders.

Until as recently as 1967, sixteen predominantly Conservative states in the Southeast enforced anti-miscegenation laws primarily between whites and nonwhite groups. The landmark Supreme Court case Loving v. Virginia that year declared such laws unconstitutional, despite more than 70% of the nation supporting them. Nearly half of the U.S. population at that time actually condoned criminal penalties for interracial marriages.

From their own perspective, Conservatives do not consider themselves as racist and embrace racial tolerance; what may appear as racism to others is seen by them as protection of tradition and heritage (Marietta, pg. 96). Many Southern Conservatives still invoke "Natural Law," believing that if God separated races globally, mixing them was not intended (Botham, pg. 134).

Opposition to interracial marriage among Conservatives often stems from a belief in "Natural Law" and cultural preservation. Liberals argue that Conservatives historically opposed equal rights for minorities, including African Americans, women, and LGBTQ+ individuals. In some Southern states, more than half of Republican populations reportedly still believe interracial marriage should be illegal (Botham, pg. 26).

Religion

Conservatives are generally religious and advocate for freedom of religion, provided these religions are traditionally accepted in their communities. The protective tribal philosophy seen in Conservative ethnic groups worldwide also characterizes Conservative religious groups. This protective stance often discourages integration with other religions, viewing them as misguided or even harmful to the community's well-being.

Monotheistic religions tend to be exclusive, regarding polytheistic beliefs as incorrect. In the United States, evangelicals, a subset of traditional Christian fundamentalists, draw from Judeo-Christian traditions as a foundation. This group constitutes a significant portion of Conservative America, vehemently opposing the rise of secularism and atheistic communism in the 1960s and 1970s (Lints, pg. 201).

Conservatism reinforces this perspective by emphasizing the Moral Community, which seeks to transcend self-interest through unity around what the community deems sacred (Lakoff, 2010, pg. 91). Throughout history, communities have achieved what many consider impossible when united for a common good—a fundamental principle behind religion. Everyone is expected to contribute to the collective whole, rather than remain isolated—a concept akin to being part of a continent rather than an isolated island (Haidt, 2006, pg. 107).

Conservatives also tend to resist change, clinging to traditional faiths and religious beliefs they were raised with, regardless of their location worldwide. They naturally defend their faith and sacred beliefs against challenges. Exposure to diverse races, cultures, and faiths in urban environments can lead individuals with Conservative traits to become more accepting, often leaning towards Liberalism compared to those in rural areas. This cultural divide explains why Northeastern and West Coast cities lean Liberal while rural Southern and Midwestern communities lean Conservative, creating a significant "cultural gap" between urban and rural America (Lakoff, 2010, pg. 394).

Sex and Marriage

Conservatives overwhelmingly support the principle that marriage should be between a natural man and woman, intended for raising a family. They view sexual activity outside of marriage as immoral, particularly if the partner is of a different race, religion, or the same sex. Homosexuality, in their view, is seen as a chosen behavior detrimental to family values. Regardless of location, Conservatives prioritize protecting the family or social group, which may be perceived by outsiders as intolerant of behaviors deemed wrong, evil, or sinful according to their faith, especially regarding sexual conduct for pleasure outside of traditional marriage.

Conservatives argue that sexual activity outside of marriage contributes significantly to issues like abortion rates in the United States (Lakoff, 2010, pg. 267). Furthermore, many children born out of wedlock grow up without fathers due to what they perceive as immoral sexual behavior. Conservatives assert that sex education should remain the responsibility of parents, not public schools. They advocate for parental review of any school-based sex education, opposing anything beyond natural biological reproduction and promoting abstinence until marriage.

Traditionally, Conservatives view sexual relationships outside heterosexual marriage, particularly across racial and religious lines, as contrary to their values and heritage. Such lifestyles are considered harmful to their way of life and against what they perceive as "God's laws" (Botham, pg. 145). Many Conservatives believe society tolerates sexual immorality excessively, using terms like "sexually active" instead of "promiscuous," a trend they attribute to Liberal influences seeking to dilute traditional Conservative values (Hayward, pg. 290).

Liberals are quick to criticize Conservative efforts to regulate marriage federally through a Constitutional amendment, arguing that such measures contradict Conservative principles of local and state control over education and other issues (Carlisle, pg. 186). They point out the inconsistency in Conservative views, where federal regulation of marriage conflicts with their preference for limited federal government involvement in citizens' lives.

Social Reform

Conservatives historically harbor concerns about a powerful central government and socialism (Farmer, pg. 19). Many argue that government involvement in social welfare implies wealth redistribution, funded by taxing those who are financially successful, thereby infringing on individual rights. Conservatives view government social programs as fostering dependency among the public, particularly among minority groups perceived to abuse entitlements. They assert that such programs, labeled as "reform" by Liberals, discourage self-reliance and incentivize laziness, hindering efforts to reintegrate people into the workforce (Farmer, pg. 40). Conservative ideology prioritizes individual freedoms, rights, and personal responsibilities over notions of equality and social or community responsibility.

An illustrative example is the Supplemental Nutrition Assistance Program (SNAP), where Conservatives advocate for cuts, citing widespread waste and fraud that they believe squanders taxpayer money. They propose additional requirements for program recipients, such as mandatory drug testing and job seminars, to promote accountability and reduce dependency. In contrast, Liberals argue for expanding such programs, citing economic hardship and the essential support they provide to families in need during difficult times.

Taxes

Conservatives prefer market-based solutions to social issues over government-run programs subsidized by taxpayer dollars, which they argue leads to bloated government (Farmer, pg. 102). They advocate for competitive marketplaces in sectors like healthcare and education, similar to the automotive and home insurance industries today. Competition driven by consumer choice, rather than government regulation, is seen as key to lowering costs and improving efficiency. Conservatives emphasize the need for a smaller government and a free market economy. They insist that all taxes on transportation and fuel should exclusively fund infrastructure improvements, such as highways, without diversion to other uses like social programs. Privately held retirement accounts, rather than government-guaranteed Social Security, are also favored as a market-driven alternative, with non-profit and religious organizations suggested to assist those unable to afford such provisions.

Conservatives support privatization because it shifts funding away from government-provided services funded by taxes, instead relying on profit-motivated private companies believed to operate more efficiently and effectively. They argue that reducing the tax burden would lower corporate costs, stimulate reinvestment, and foster economic growth (Wilson, pg. 381). Conservatives firmly assert that wealth is acquired through hard work and discipline, deeming the redistribution of wealth via taxes to support those perceived as less industrious as immoral and unacceptable (Wilson, pg. 120).

Wealth

For Conservatives, wealth represents more than mere financial resources—it serves as the bedrock of societal strength and resilience, enabling not just survival but flourishing across communities and nations. Wealth plays a pivotal role in ensuring fundamental aspects of human life, including providing shelter, sustenance, education, and the means to enjoy life's finer aspects. Beyond these essential needs, wealth empowers families and nations to safeguard themselves against a myriad of threats, both internal to the family and community and externally from threats nationally and from abroad.

Internally, wealth facilitates robust law enforcement measures that combat crime and maintain public safety. It supports initiatives aimed at reducing societal vulnerabilities to criminal activities, thereby fostering safer and more secure communities. Moreover, wealth underpins efforts to counteract terrorism, a persistent global threat that targets the very fabric of societal stability. Agencies like the Department of Homeland Security exemplify this protective function, tirelessly working to prevent terrorist attacks on American soil and mitigate threats overseas (Bolt, pg. 433).

Externally, wealth translates into military capability and diplomatic influence, essential components in safeguarding national interests and projecting power globally. Economic prosperity enables investment in cutting-edge defense technologies, training for military personnel, and strategic alliances with international partners, all of which bolster national security. This capability not only defends against external aggression but also promotes stability in regions critical to global peace.

In essence, Conservatives view wealth not just as a means of personal prosperity but as a cornerstone of societal and national strength. It forms the economic backbone that sustains and fortifies communities, enabling them to confront challenges, protect liberties, and uphold the values that define their way of life.

Through prudent stewardship and strategic allocation of resources, Conservatives argue that wealth becomes a force multiplier, enhancing resilience and ensuring a secure future for generations to come.

Moreover, wealth isn't just about military or police power; it empowers economic prowess—the ability to drive essential societal developments. Conservatives argue that wealth is generated through human endeavor and drives all other societal achievements. This economic power translates into social and political influence, enabling technological advancements, scientific breakthroughs, and medical innovations crucial for societal progress and resilience.

Conservatives assert that military strength is directly tied to economic prosperity, emphasizing that a nation's prosperity and resilience hinge on economic freedom, resourcefulness, and diligent effort. They caution against complacency and dependence on taxing the wealthy within society, warning that such practices can erode economic vitality and weaken once powerful nations into decline.

The Left

Liberals

The origins of Liberalism come from ancient times where man desired liberty during times of slavery and freedom to live his own way during times of oppressive rule. These Classic Liberal ideas are the foundation of liberty and modern democracy in the 1700's; this was the "Age of Reason" where people strove for political liberty as well as a capitalistic society with economic freedoms for all (Green, pg. xxiii). Classic Liberalism is also the foundation of the modern Conservative Republican, Libertarian and Tea Party movements. These organizations evolved over time from the writings of Thomas Paine, Benjamin Franklin and Thomas Jefferson (Farmer, pg. 35).

Contemporary Liberal issues are quite a bit different from Classic Liberalism and should not be confused with those ideologies of basic human freedoms and "natural rights." In the United States, Contemporary Liberals or modern Social Liberals claim different and broader modern day rights and freedoms. They look at themselves as "Progressives" that have driven change and improvements for social justice progressively over the years with a focus on what they perceive as human and animal rights and freedoms. These rights range from the right of animals to be free from cruelty, women's rights to have an abortion, equal rights for women and minorities in the workplace and the legalization of recreational drugs.

These issues of liberty in the United States from the days of slavery until the modern time issues of abortion, healthcare and poverty have had slow but decisive progress over the years. It is hard for Liberals to understand why the Conservatives "care" so much for the unborn yet show much "less concern" for those who are born yet suffer and are in need (Farmer, pg. 54). Why is it immoral to abort the fetus yet not moral and right to enable the government to help protect the needy that slip through the cracks? Although there already is plenty of help offered through independent social and religious charitable entities, tens of thousands of people still live impoverished lives while so many live in prosperity. Many Conservatives believe that these poor are simply freeloaders that are dependent on handouts. They are poor because of laziness, lack of motivation, discipline and crime and that it is immoral to give free handouts to them as it promotes dependency.

Personal protection and personal provision that is provided for by the Federal Government is the primary Liberal progressive ambition. These are costly appeals that require a larger and more costly government that provides healthcare and equality of educational for everyone, protection of the environment and protection from bigotry against women, minorities, gays and the poor (Lakoff, 2010, pg. 21). Liberals also press for continued separation of Church and State and freedom "from" religion such as in cases like prayer in school which can in their minds oppress those of dissimilar faiths than those around them.

The Left

Over the years Conservative religiously biased laws such as blue laws, prohibition and biased laws against sexual acts and preference as well as interracial marriage have progressively been overturned. These changes that gradually came were simply attempts to correct the most blatant injustice of the moment and then move on to the next one. These injustices in some cases only became apparent or possible to address when a previous injustice had been removed; for example the emancipation of the slaves and then the black man's right to vote which followed with the woman's right to vote (Carlisle, pg. 427). The pursuit of greater equality and of identity is very much depended on the particular circumstances a society is dealing with at the time.

These Liberal vs Conservative issues have not necessarily been Democrat vs Republican issues as depending on the circumstance, each will vary in time and place. These are the Left against the Right issues with the left being the Liberals concern for social justice and the right being the Conservatives concern for family and national traditional values. The Liberal concern is primarily for the weak in society, those in who are viewed as underprivileged in relation to others, including not only humans but animals, nature and the environment. These are unjustified inequalities that need to be addressed or eliminated in order to correct injustices that often are challenged by Conservatives due to the impact on politics, local businesses and the economy.

Liberals believe in a government that provides equal opportunity and equality for all and tries to alleviate social wrongs and protect the civil liberties and human rights of its people (Carlisle, pg. 199). They believe that the responsibility of the government is to guarantee that none of its people are in need and that government policies should emphasize the need for the government to solve social difficulties.

In the United States just after the Civil War, voting was limited only to white adult males who owned property. Liberals began addressing this issue and after great debate pushed through the Fifteenth Amendment to the United States Constitution which States that no one can deny a citizen the right to vote based on "race, color, or previous condition of servitude." It is interesting to note that at that time, it was the more Liberal Northern Republicans that pushed for this progressive Amendment to the Constitution. This was against the will of the Conservative Southern Democrats who wanted to maintain their traditions that enabled their plantations to flourish under slavery.

Reform first came when the requirement to own property in order to vote was abolished and then then the right to vote was given to black men in 1870. Finally the right to vote was officially offered to women in 1919 with passing of the Nineteenth Amendment which prohibits voting based on gender (Green, pg. 1119). This was also led by the more Liberal Republican Party and opposed by Conservative Southern Democrats.

Similarly gays in the United States had to hide their true identity and remain "underground" in order to avoid oppression. Over time, the demand by Liberals for an end to laws prohibiting homosexual and certain heterosexual acts reduce this persecution. In 1969, the birth of the gay rights movement began with the Stonewall Riots in New York City (Green, pg. 462). This success was followed by the call for domestic partner rights to be equivalent to those enjoyed by hetero-sexual married couples. The *Obergefell vs Hodges* landmark Supreme Court case legalizing gay marriage with a 5 to 4 decision in 2015 and was highly contested by Conservatives. Likewise in 1973 the Supreme Court in the *Roe vs Wade* ruled that prohibiting abortion was unconstitutional was another achievement for the progressives

Stereotypes of Liberals can entertain words like intellectual, environmentalist, gay, young, hippies, pro-choice, pro-union, pro-gun control, multicultural, progressive, pro-science, cultured, pro-free expression, for the common people, media friendly, pro-labor, New Englander and pro-separation of church and State. Many of these can have negative connotations such as, weak on defense, anti-business, communist, socialist, anarchist, support higher taxes and big government, support redistribution of wealth and anti-rich. Again, most stereotypes falsely characterize and overly simplify various perspectives of a group; however as in all stereotypes, there is some amount of truth to these words.

Abortion

Generally speaking, most Liberals support the legalization of abortion and the termination of unwanted pregnancies during the first trimester. They believe that especially for those under the poverty line, the cost for these abortions should be handled as all health care should be for the poor and be covered by tax payer's dollars. Having an abortion is a right to privacy that is covered under the "Due Process" clause of the 14th Amendment.

This amendment States: *"No State shall make or enforce any law which shall **abridge the privileges or immunities of citizens** of the United States; nor shall any State **deprive any person of life, liberty, or property,** without **due process of law...**"*

Personhood is not necessarily given to the unborn child wherein the problem in interpreting the 14th Amendment comes (Alcorn, pg. 76).

Liberals believe that many of these privileges and liberties are "unnamed rights" or rights not Stated in the Constitution or the Bill of Rights. These are "natural rights" such as the right to marry, to raise children or other privacy matters that the Ninth Amendment relates to; this is the "right to be let alone" as eluded to in the Four Amendment.

This right to privacy is to be:

"Secure in their persons, houses, papers, and effects"

This is a law that protects one from unwanted intrusive meddling in one's personal matters. Privacy is an individual freedom to engage in specific activities or expose one's selves to various types of experiences including specific sexual acts, sexual preference and if necessary, abortions. This right to privacy however is historically defined narrowly by the courts as relating to one's sexuality, marriage, maternity and in raising children in the home. To Liberals, denial of abortion rights is "enforced motherhood" and violates the Thirteenth Amendment's abolition of involuntary servitude and that the woman's liberty is at stake.

This amendment States: "*There shall be neither slavery nor involuntary servitude...*"

The Supreme Court also observed that: "*Women do not lose the Constitutional rights when they marry*" (Green, pg. 854).

Abortion rights or Pro-choice activists also believe that life does not begin at conception as Pro-life activists do and that a woman has the right to protect her livelihood and financial condition by having a "Right to Choose" an abortion. Pro-choice advocates believe that a fetus is not a legal "person" and that the woman's rights to freedom are the primary focus; a fetus in the first trimester cannot be considered as a legal person because it is not "self-aware" and therefore not a whole person. The unborn according to the court in *Roe vs Wade*, have never been recognized by law as persons in the whole sense (Green, pg. 874).

In many countries today, an abortion is morally acceptable even if the fetus is considered as a person and has a "right to life" as the woman has the right to control the life-support functions of her own body. To many, the semantics of terms "personhood" or "life" that are used in the arguments are only rhetoric that drives both sides of the argument.

In truth it can be argued that if the fetus is allowed to live, it will become a human being and a "person." It may be that this person may make a mark on their society for the positive or negative in the future; the abortion will prevent this "person" from ever existing. However, this thinking is a slippery slope in that if a law is written to apply protections to someone who "would have" or "could have been," then the morning after pill would also become illegal along with abortion. This then also could apply to someone who would have been if not for contraception and make that illegal as well. To add to this then of course, oral sex would also prevent this "person" from being and become illegal; then again not forgetting that "abstinence" its self prevents a person from being. Furthermore, the prevention of natural sexual instincts and desires that have been set in motion would also then prevent a life from becoming and become illegal; this all becomes quite absurd.

To the Liberal, the question really is "does the woman have the right to terminate the pregnancy to protect her rights and freedoms?" Conservatives many times say that humans are not to "play God." How then does an adult soldier have the moral right to kill another adult enemy combatant in a war to protect the homeland's "way of life?" How is it also moral to put to death a murderer on death row for taking the life of another? Why is it morally right to shoot and kill an intruder for coming into your home? Is that not "playing God?" Why is there this hostility toward a woman and a two month old fetus that no one else knows exists? The soldier, the burglar and the murderer all may have family and people who have been attached to them and depended on them for decades. Yet there is little concern for these men by Conservatives and great concern for the unknown fetus. Who has the greater right of "personhood," the two month old fetus or the woman who is choosing to have the abortion who otherwise would be forced into motherhood and deeper poverty against her will? The Supreme Court ruled in *Roe vs Wade* that the liberty of a woman is at stake here and that an abortion is her right (Green, pg. 854).

To Conservatives, Liberal's belief in the right to have an abortion seems to conflict with the Liberal belief in animal rights and that animals at times are held to a higher level of importance than a human unborn baby (Alcorn, pg. 79). In addition, Liberals tend to be against the Death Penalty and that the right to life is the most important right that a human can have, yet Liberals support the millions of abortions that take place every year; as high as 1.7 million abortions in 1990 alone but decreased to around 1 million a year

2014. To the Conservative, this in fact seems to show that Liberals hold a criminal, a thief or a terrorist to a higher level of importance than that of an innocent human baby.

Liberals point out that there seems to be a contradiction in how Conservatives view this issue. There currently is an extremely high infant-mortality rate in the United States primarily because of the lack of adequate prenatal care for poor mothers. Doctors many times are prevented from offering prenatal care to poor mothers because "this service is outside the scope of the Federal funded program" (Goldstein, pg. 81). With that said, Conservatives have never been in favor of government programs that provide prenatal care (Lakoff, 2010, pg. 25). Traditionally they have tried to eliminate existing programs that have been shown to lower infant mortality rate as costly programs paid for by tax payer's dollars. In 2015, the United States ranked 38th in the world in infant mortality with 5 deaths per 1,000 births. Liberals ask; if the Conservatives are so concerned with the lives of these babies, why do they not support these programs? The answer may simply be that the majority of these infant mortality deaths are with poor minority mothers; rich white mothers do not have these same issues.

Roe vs Wade was overturned by the Supreme Court in 2024 due to Conservative Justices being added to the Court by President Donald J. Trump.

Affirmative Action

In the 1960's, it was clear that blacks in the United States were clearly an underclass and something had to be done in this oppressive and racist society. Liberals pushed through the Affirmative Action programs which came out of the Civil Rights Act of 1964 and helped many blacks and minorities to rise out of poverty in the 1970's and were getting better education. This gave those who had qualities of potential to have opportunities that they otherwise would not have had. This was a form of restitution, to give compensation to blacks for the atrocities of slavery in the past. This gave priority to minority rights over individual rights.

By the 1980's, Conservatives however were pushing back and wanted an end to Affirmative Action as to them it was no longer necessary. In 1983, in the *Bob Jones University vs The United States*, the Supreme Court ruled that if Bob Jones University wanted to keep its tax-exempt status, it had to abide by non-discriminative admission policies or forfeit its federal aid program; this was a big win for Liberals and Affirmative Action (Carlisle, pg. 8). In 2023, the Supreme Court weakened affirmative action by ending race-conscious admission programs into Universities across the country.

Animal Rights

Many Liberals believe that animals in general should have rights similar to humans, being protected from harm and abuse (Farmer, pg. 108). Liberals assert that animals should not be considered as personal property or used unethically as research subjects, enslaved for human entertainment or beasts of burden, especially in societies that are advanced (Regan, pg. 180). Many vegans feel that killing animals for food or use their flesh for products such as leather or furs is unethical and cruel.

Women and children are more likely to sympathize with animal rights than adult men because they have a greater tendency to be compassionate and nurturing and men are less so and love to hunt. Liberals believe that animals that humans exploit are not just a part of this world that we live in, they are aware of it as well. What happens to them matters to them; all having individual needs that are biological and social needs, much like humans they have and share both pleasure and pain. All human and animal life has a basic moral right to respectful treatment and should not be treated as if they are a resource for others. One creature's greater capacity to cognitive awareness does not give that creature a greater inherent value than a creature with lesser cognitive awareness (Regan, pg. xvi-xviii).

"People for the Ethical Treatment of Animals" or PETA is a left wing Liberal group whose focus has been on cruelty to animals. Industrial cattle farming is just one of the issues Liberals are concerned with in respect to the welfare of animals. Replicated trophy-hunting, raising animals in furs farms, product testing on animals as well as the trade of exotic animals and the factory farming of bears in China for bile are just

52

some of the atrocities animals must endure. For many years sharks have been killed for their fins as well in Asia for unproven health remedies.

To many Conservatives and Liberals, PETA is extreme with a goal of total animal liberation with the intent of abolishing firs, meat, dairy products and even zoos and aquariums, making millions of dollars in the process (Baier, pg. 176).

Capital Punishment

Quite a few Liberals are opposed to capital punishment as an eye for an eye to them is barbarian and that they believe that rehabilitation may be possible for some criminals; to them, the Death Penalty should be abolished. Likewise the Liberals will remind the Conservatives that many on Death Row have been found to be innocent and have been released while some have died by capital punishment and found to be innocent too late; every execution has the risk of killing yet an another innocent life. In addition the Death Penalty is inhumane and considered as a cruel and unusual punishment and that imprisonment is the fitting punishment for murder. It has not been shown to be a deterrent as criminals do no normally analyze the outcome of their crime (Lakoff, 2010, pg. 208).

With over 40% of those on Death Row being black and only about 12% of the population of the United States as black, Liberals often see racism as a contributing factor. Research also shows that whites are more likely to support Capital Punishment when it is mostly applied to blacks (Nathanson, pg. 54). Also most of the "first world" countries such as Canada and all of Europe have abolished Capital Punishment with the exception of the United States. Liberals believe that the right to life is the most important right that a human can have and that capital punishment and the Death Penalty desecrates this most valuable human right in the most egregious way.

Conservatives point out that Liberals are weak on crime and see it contradictory that they would support the slaughter of millions of innocent babies and yet be so sensitive to criminal's rights on death row who are repulsive and evil murderers.

Constitution Interpretation

The Liberal non-originalist such as Justice Harry Blackmun and Justice William Brennan believe that the original text of the Constitution did not invalidate offensive, oppressive, undemocratic and sectarian laws. They understand that the framers of the Constitution in Philadelphia indicated that they did not want their "specific" intentions to control interpretation. To them the founders of the Constitution did not leave detailed deliberations on what their original intent was allowing the Constitution to evolve to match more tolerant understandings on matters.

These matters are things such as the equal treatment of people of color, women, the LGBT community and other minorities and ethnic groups across America. Instead they favor giving more weight to precedent over the years, to learn from consequences of decisions made in the past on previous interpretations as well as what is understood as natural law. Sometimes non-originalists favor decisions that are deemed as "wrong" by Conservative originalist because it supports stability and promotes the public good. The larger purpose of the Constitution was to protection the liberty of the American people, whoever they may be.

Crime

Liberals believe that much of crime occurs due to the social injustice of being poor and lacking an education. Some people turn to crime due to poverty and not having the ability to improve their situation with honest hard work. To them, they are condemned to live in poverty and that the cards are stacked against them especially once they have a criminal record. Only in eliminating these social conditions that clearly correlate with and foster crime can we reduce crime (Farmer, pg. 108). These injustices as far as minorities are concerned are often the result of pure prejudice.

Rehabilitation of criminals for many Liberals is possible and should be addressed financially by the government rather than building more prisons. Liberals consider compassion as a primary driver in how they live and that we must have compassion and empathy for even the hardened criminals. They stress the importance of individual human rights and that it is better to let some criminals go than to falsely imprison or even put to death innocent people (Nathanson, pg. 12).

Red and Blue

Many Liberals believe that the Criminal Justice System is troubled with human oversight and that human rights need to be protected. To them this is clearly seen in prejudice with an inequality of treatment between race and class where prisons are overwhelmingly filled with black and Hispanic men vs white men. Currently black men make up about 13 percent of drug users but 46 percent are convicted for drug offenses. In some areas of the nation one out of every three black men can expect to go to prison some time in their lifetime. Minorities are more likely to be arrested and convicted than whites and if convicted, minorities are more likely to be given harsher sentences than whites.

According to the Huffington (Post Huffpost Crime 10/22/2014), as of 2013, Russia had 475 inmates per 100,000 Russian residents while China has 121 inmates per 100,000 residents. In the United States, many States, mainly southern States, have much more with Louisiana at almost double the Russian rate at 893 per 100,000 residents and Mississippi right behind at 717 and Alabama at 650. Oklahoma and Texas are right behind them with 648 and 601 respectively; all are significantly higher than both Russia and China. During the Cold war and even today, Russia and China's were and still are frequently targets in the United States, in respect to political prisoners of which many were Christian pastors according to the press and many religious organizations.

Today, a high percentage of the prisoners in the United States and especially southern States, are in prison as a result of untreated mental illness or drug abuse with most of them black men. Conservatives in general have no tolerance for crime, especially for career offenders and violent crimes and consistently search for the resources to hold these criminals responsible for their actions.

Drugs

Liberals tend to support the legalization of recreational drugs such as marijuana and some even look at these drugs as beneficial and as medicine. The list of recreational drugs or "soft drugs" includes tobacco, alcohol, marijuana and hallucinogenic mushrooms. The harder and more dangerous drugs are drugs such as Heroin, Opium, LSD, Amphetamines and Cocaine. Basically for Liberals, if you choose to use soft drugs you need to be responsible for your actions to ensure no one is harmed. The harder drugs have historically been proven to be detrimental to society.

What is interesting is that it was the Liberal Progressive temperance movement that banned alcohol in the 1920's. Temperance advocates did not always stress the prohibiting of alcohol. Once the use of alcohol was openly associated with social problems such as poverty and opium addiction, the temperance movement by the 1920's made it their main focus. The temperance movement often went hand in hand with other social reform movements like female suffrage, the right to vote being concerned with social issues. Many

Conservatives, especially the libertarians, point out that Liberals have not really changed and continue to push for big government that meddles in peoples private matters.

As for the harder drugs, many Liberals stand with the Conservatives and support the War on Drugs. When it comes to soft drugs (Bertram, pg. 93), some Liberals believe that recreational drugs such as cannabis, psilocybin mushrooms, LSD, and ecstasy should be regulated as semi-controlled substances and taxed just as tobacco and alcohol is today. This tax can be used as a way to raise money for governmental finance of health programs for addicts and a way to control and prevent adolescent abuse.

As far as the War on Drugs, even under the Liberal Clinton Administration, this war continued just as meticulously as under the Bush presidencies both in Latin America and with the crackdowns on medical marijuana dispensaries in the U. S. For many Liberals, this War on Drugs is a huge attack on personal liberty as well as on most other civil liberties (Bertram, pg. 142). Even the Liberal Obama Administration did not offer to address these issues other than allowing some States like Colorado to legalize marijuana under his watch. Instead of pushing to legalize it federally, they suggest that we wait and see what happens in the "experiments."

Liberals argue that prisons are full of drug offenders, many for non-violent crimes that have been based on the Conservatives "three strikes you're out" philosophy (Lakoff, 2010, pg. 148). Most of these lives are being ruined without the opportunity to make amends because of their prison sentences and records. Liberals also believe that the government, the military and private prisons have made a lot of money from tax payer dollars and from the seizure of private property which is argued as necessary to facilitate the War on Drugs. The United States only makes up about five percent of the world's population but holds about twenty-five percent of the world's prisoners. Even back in the 1990's, the Surgeon General suggested that legalization of some drugs might in fact "reduce our crime rate" (Bertram, pg. 160). As of 2024, many States across the country have legalized marijuana.

Economics

When it comes to economics, Liberals generally support an increase in the federal minimum wage to help the poor keep income in step with inflation and keep millions above the poverty line (Lakoff, 2010, pg. 203). They also in most cases support labor unions and the right to organize to help the middle class economically. Most Liberals also oppose trade deals that export jobs that in their opinion make corporations richer at the expense of American workers. In general, most Liberals support putting a stop to tax breaks for these companies that export these jobs overseas. Many of the poor in the United States are immigrants and Liberals see the need for immigration reform to safeguard these low-income workers from being taken advantage of by corporations.

Most Liberals would support the "Buffett Rule" that would force millionaires to pay equally when it comes to taxes by applying a minimum tax rate of 30 percent on people making over a million dollars a year (Miroff, pg. 58). Liberals believe that government should provide more services to the less fortunate and that this expanded role for the government includes these services that are many times called "entitlement programs" that should be supported by taxes on the wealthy. These include programs for the less fortunate such as Social Security, Medicaid, Medicare, Food Stamps, Universal Healthcare, as well as free public education and unemployment benefits.

The Liberals believe that the middle class has essentially collapsed economically since the 2008 Wall Street crash. Wealth and income inequality as well as childhood poverty is greater in the United States than any other first world nation. They argue that the inflation-adjusted income for the average worker is far less last year than one made 40 years ago with the female worker making less today than she made 10 years ago. Liberals believe that the way to fix this inequality is to reform the tax code to be fair, to be based on the workers income and remove loopholes that allow wealthy corporations to bank overseas and hide money from the IRS (Miroff, pg. 58).

Education and Children

Liberals are united in support for governmental legislation that provides equal opportunity education for all children and promotes multiculturalism, political correctness and religious tolerance (Carlisle, pg. 622). They also believe that all public educational institutions that are funded by the government, educate students under the same standardized testing process. According to Liberals, in the late 1990's, the United States led the world with the highest percentage of people to graduate from college but today it is in 12th place worldwide (Stone, pg. 454).

These institutions were virtually tuition free but today college is unaffordable for most; those who do complete college many times have huge loans to pay off. Liberals support legislation that would help make higher education more affordable and help restore America's competitive edge in the global marketplace. To the Liberal, government needs to support programs that help disadvantaged kids so that they too can have the same opportunities as other children. Conservatives feel that this is robbing from the rich to give to the poor and is immoral; to them the Department of Education should be abolished (Lakoff, 2010, pg. 229).

Liberals tend to oppose Charter Schools that receive public funding through taxes but are run independently of the public school system. Many of these schools are partially funded with grants and donations from corporations and operate without the influence of the teachers unions. Liberals believe that the Charter School operators are in it for the money, funded by public education funds but also through external entities. This in effect undermines the public school system and gives an unfair advantage to the students that attend these schools and seems to have patterns of segregation along racial, ethnic and socioeconomic lines (Wilson, pg. 355).

School vouchers are also an issue with Liberals where public education funds are given back to parents who are able to redirect this money towards private school of their own choice or reimburse home schooling expenses. Liberals see this as taking taxes that were initially intended as funding for the public school system away from the schools which undermines the ability of the public schools from providing a better education (Wilson, pg. 352). In the Southern States during efforts to desegregate the public school system in the 1960's, school vouchers were used to continue segregation ending in many public schools closing for lack of funds.

Energy

Most Liberals talk "green" and truly want to stop global warming but that does not necessarily cause them from driving their Lincolns and SUV's. They understand the need to become energy independent but that does not warrant more drilling on the Gulf Coast, running an oil line across the U.S. for Canadian oil or digging more coal mines. Liberals have not only been concerned about global warming and acid rain but also are bringing attention to the rate at which we are depleting our mineral resources and that alternative fuels that are renewable are necessary. Renewable energy sources such as solar, wind and ethanol are the main contenders to replace coal, natural gas and crude oil which according to many scientists are the root cause for greenhouse gasses that creates global warming. Nuclear energy was not an option for most Liberals ever since the Three Mile Island accident in Pennsylvania in 1979 and the Chernobyl disaster of 1986 (Green, pg. 374).

Liberals contest that the regulations that are in place that control pollution from industry as well as mining and drilling for mineral sources of energy were created for a reason. As they say, regulations are "written in blood," something somewhere happened that caused these rules to be written. These were events such as the huge oil spill of the coast of Santa Barbara California in 1969 (Farmer, pg. 108) and the 2010 Deepwater Horizon oil spill in the Gulf that became a huge environmental hazard. The carcinogenic fuel additive MTBE from refineries also contaminated drinking water supplies in the 1990's and EPA regulations helped control these spills and contaminations. Over time these events were forgotten and industry in an attempt to throw off high costs and regulatory burdens try to get the rules changed.

Many Conservatives want to eliminate the Department of Energy and the EPA because of their hindrance to industrial profits. In fact the Conservative George H. W. Bush administration pulled out of the Kyoto Accords stating that carbon dioxide was not a pollutant (Green, pg. 374). Restricting U.S. industrial emissions while trying to compete with China, the world's biggest polluter causes serious harm to the economy; Liberal's fight back recalling the reasons for the regulations in the first place and the need for regulating industry (Lakoff, 2010, pg. 415).

Environment

Liberals in general support the undertaking to protect of the environment even though in may mean job loss for some. They see protecting the environment as not only a major practical investment but a moral mission for their children's future and that Global Warming is a real and present danger to the world's future populations (Lakoff, 2010, pg. 328). Liberals feel that regulating corporations in prevention of pollution into the drinking water, the soil and the air through the EPA and other governmental agencies is the best way to combat pollution. Relaxing regulations on these large corporations would only bring back these dark days in exchange for big profits.

Liberals believe that economic gain is not as important as the damage that industry can do without regulations through visual disfiguring and damage to the environment. An example of this as stated before is the oil rigs off the Gulf Coast and the increased risk of damage to the environment from oil spills as seen in April of 2010. Another example is the huge freshwater aquafer under Los Angeles that is unusable due to World War II era perchlorate rocket fuel (Steinzor, pg. 128). These chemicals are water soluble and are difficult if not impossible to remove from irrigation and drinking water. If not enforced, problems like those with Flint Michigan's contamination of lead in the drinking water when switching to the river's corrosive water occur as government and corporations try to find ways to save money.

These Liberals or "progressives" also recognize that great progress has been made since the seventies when the Great Lakes were so polluted that they were almost void of fish and when southern California air pollution was an immense health hazard. Unity with nature is a protective and nurturance stance as one has empathy with nature similar to how someone desires to care for their children (Lakoff, 2010, pg. 210). The desire to protect nature from pollution is the same desire as to protect ones child from harm. Part of the EPA's job is to protect the land, water and air if necessary as part of the Endangered Species Act of 1973 to protect endangered life.

Liberals believe that a reformed tax code could support an expanded role of the government with stronger environmental laws and regulations on industries that protect the environment through taxes on industry. Conservatives charge that this would come at the expense of individual civil liberties and property rights and limit corporate profits (Farmer, pg. 108).

Euthanasia

Many Liberals, who in what may seem to be contradictory, don't agree with the Death Penalty but believe in assisted suicide and euthanasia for those who are suffering terminal illnesses. For some reason many that would see it ethical to help a sick parent die, would not see it ethical to execute someone who tortured and murdered people by burying his victims alive. In 1997, the U.S. Supreme Court ruled that the States have the right to prohibit or allow physician-assisted suicide and that there is no Constitutional right to assisted suicide. Today four out of fifty States have legalized physician-assisted suicide; Washington, Oregon, California and Vermont. The Washington State the "Death with Dignity Act" was passed in 2008 by approximately 59% for and 41% against (Keegan, pg. 29).

Many Liberals being nonreligious people who believe that life begins and ends on earth emphasize that the woman alone decides if her unborn child lives or if the pregnancy is terminated. These same people also believe that the elderly sick and terminally ill along with those closest to them, have the final say when their lives should end and have the "right to die with dignity" (Green, pg. 865). If it would be inhumane to let ones pet suffer in horrible anguish, why would anyone allow one's loved one to endure such agony? To them ones religious beliefs, although they should be highly respected, should not dictate another's personal decisions of life and death.

Government Spending

Liberals in the past have passed massive government spending on social programs while they have had the predisposition to try to reduce spending on the nation's military. Liberals tend to be federalist and prefer more regulation to protect against what they see to be greed that promotes injustice to the poor and the working class and harm to the environment. Liberals prefer these government services such as free universal healthcare to be provided by the government to all citizens through tax payers dollars and see this as a moral obligation of the government (Lakoff, 2010, pg. 185). Social Security and Welfare supplies a safeguard for the countries unfortunate and poor; cutting funding to these systems would most certainly make many people to suffer as a result.

Liberals tout that although the United States has the highest GDP per capita in the world that the U.S. government according to The Heritage Foundation data, spends far less than the world average government spending per capita. The CIA World Factbook States out of other first world governments the U.S. spends approximately $10,000 per person on government services compared with Norway with about $41,000 per person. The U.S. was 25th in spending according to the International Monetary Fund with a tax burden percent of Gross National Product of 25% compared to Norway's at 43% and Denmark's at 48%.

In 2012, the Federal Government reduced the growth of spending and the deficit shrank to 7.6% of GDP. U.S. revenues from taxes and other sources are lower, as a percentage of GDP than those of most other countries. However the wars in Afghanistan and in Iraq shifted costs from civilian to military costs with a direct cost of these wars being over $900 billion and contributed to a growth in the budget (IBP, pg. 23)

Gun Control

The Liberal interpretation of the Second Amendment is that the authors meant this as the right for States to form militias and not for individuals to bear arms for self-defense and even hunting. In fact in 1876, the Supreme Courts first interpretation of the Second Amendment in *The United States vs Cruikshank* was that this amendment was for the Federal Government and not the States, let alone individuals (Spitzer, pg. 72).

To most Liberals however, this does not take away the freedom to own weapons of various sorts, especially for sport or for hunting; the emphasis is mainly on semi-automatic guns designed for warfare and hand guns designed to be concealed. The focus of gun control is to control crime and to ensure that felons and the mentally ill do not obtain guns and to keep weapons out of school property and government buildings (Garry, pg. 57-58). It is the interpretation of the Second Amendment that is in question here; for them, statistics clearly show the need for more control.

Liberals point out that unlike most of the "advanced" countries in the world, the United States has relatively few restrictions on gun ownership. It is the widespread ownership of hand guns that is the root cause of homicide with handguns. Thousands of wrongful deaths occur each year by crime, suicide, and the accidental death of children (Spitzer, pg. 180). Although it is often hard to prove, advocates of gun control argue that studies show that States with stricter gun control laws have lower death rates due to accidental death and suicide. These restrictions are open carrying regulations, mandating gun locks, waiting periods to take ownership after purchase and background checks.

Liberals do not understand why someone who opposes gun control because it infringes on individual freedom would at the same time oppose the individual freedoms sought for such as gay rights and to be free to have an abortion (Lakoff, 2010, pg. 199).

Healthcare

Liberals believe that personal health should never be reliant on upon one's financial income and that the government through taxation should intervene to provide that service; access to affordable universal healthcare must be given to all. Almost every wealthy industrialized country in the world provides universal healthcare except for the United States. Conservatives strongly reject this notion and believe that Healthcare should be provided by private enterprise in a competitive market to keep costs down. However Liberals point out that as in the case of South Africa and the HIV AIDS epidemic that if not for government intervention, the private sector would have never been involved with the research. There would have been no profit in providing medications for the poor and the government stepped in to help the cause as private enterprise would not (Cutler, pg. 85).

Red and Blue

The United States government presently spends more money per person on healthcare than any other first world country. According to the CIA World Factbook the total U.S. government spending on healthcare both public and private, rose from 9. 0% of GDP in 1980 to 17. 9% in 2010; this spending has declined slightly to 16.4% of GDP in 2013 according to current OECD data. The private enterprise multi institutional insurance process in the U.S. that is supposed to reduce costs through competition has actually worked against most Americans. According to Liberals, this "competitive" process has actually made medical supply and pharmaceutical corporations some of the wealthiest companies in the world on the taxpayers' dollars.

Harvard's David Cutler States that about one quarter of the United States healthcare cost is associated with administration costs, which is far higher than in any other country. Countries such as Canada and other European countries have a single tier payment system through the government that utilizes less administration and simplifies the payment process (Cutler, pg. 118). The next issue is that brand name drugs and medical equipment cost much more in the U.S. than elsewhere in the world and doctors earn much more than in other countries. Research costs for medications and certification of medical equipment can be enormous and it takes time to recoup these costs (Cutler, pg. 45). Without cost control, these companies are free to make huge profits at the expense of those who need help.

In most markets, competition is beneficial in keeping costs down, however the lowest prices for medications and medical equipment and physician costs are found in government plans. It has been shown that people living in the United States that have unequal income distribution die at a younger age than people who have a more equal income distribution in countries like Sweden and northern Europe (Cutler, pg. 55).

Liberals also point out that these same countries that have government run healthcare systems have cost much less than the system in the United States. Part of this cost is that Americans receive much more medical care than necessary, most likely due the desire for financial gain rather than need. In the United States for example you are far more likely to have open heart surgery than in Canada for a heart attack yet the life expectancy after a heart attack is the same for the two countries (Cutler, pg. 58).

Human Rights

Liberals believe that human rights can only be achieved through economic equality and that systems based on legal rights cannot protect the people alone. Liberals consider themselves to be open minded and rather than only treating religion as sacred, many believe that equality in the form of civil rights and human right should be treated as sacred as well (Haidt, 2013, pg. 204). People need rights to protect them from those who have power and would abuse them. Government power in the proper hands can do good things however the power of the government in wrong hands can undermine people's liberty and rights especially when it supports the interests of big business. The Liberals have long pursued to bring down the status of the wealthy and elevate the status of the maligned whether they are poor or oppressed because of race, sexuality, religion, health or age.

Conservatives naturally address what they feel is right and what is wrong, however Liberalism by its own definition is tolerant. Liberals embrace things like diversity and inclusion and naturally incorporate those of various opinions. Liberals feel that Conservatives take away people's rights when they hold to values that are obsolete or foreign to their surroundings. They believe that the preservation of government power is necessary to enforce the civil rights and human rights of the people (Lakoff, 2010, pg. 150).

Immigration

Liberals tend to support amnesty and a freeze on deportation of undocumented immigrants and in general celebrate diversity (Haidt, 2013, pg. 193). They also propose presenting a pathway to citizenship for those with no criminal record and who have lived in the U.S. for a longer period of time. Most undocumented immigrants are spouses of U.S. citizens with children who are also citizens which if brought in through the legal process would possibly send one parent home to the country of origin and separate the family for up to ten years. This discourages undocumented immigrants from going through the standard legal process. Also legal fees and legal representation must be paid for by the individual making the ability of the poor almost impossible to be legally processed. Conservative argue that whether we provide a pathway to citizenship or not, those who have entered the U.S. illegally should not be given a preference over those who wait and go through the proper process (Bush, pg. x)

Many young people that are born in a foreign country but are raised in the United States are deported to their country of origin because of minor drug offenses without knowing the language or knowing any relatives. Most of them end up in prisons abroad for much of their lives or in gangs in countries such as Guatemala and El Salvador as they have no families other than those who were deported before them. All of these issues are raised by Liberals as issues of concern with the need for immigration reform as a priority for them as issues of human rights (Lakoff, 2010, pg. 188).

Liberty, Privacy and Property

Liberals support the concept of Liberty and freedom to a point. When it comes to public health, regulations on the food industry to prevent endangering the health of the public by eating unhealthy food or public drinking water have to be put into place and enforced. Liberals believe that many aspects of human activity need to be monitored or controlled to some extent in order to also prevent public health and harm issues. This may include such regulation as rules on the sale of unpasteurized dairy products and saturated fats as well as drinking water regulations on fluoride and chlorine levels or the lack of these chemicals.

Much of the Liberal approach to liberty is more akin to equality and the freedom to be who you are; human rights equality is to have equal rights under the law (Lakoff, 2010, pg. 151).   In the past this meant equality for disadvantaged groups of society such as slaves and freedom and a woman's right to property and to vote.   Today this freedom is for equal pay for women and other minorities in society as well as equal rights for gays and lesbians for marriage and the associated benefits.   For this reason many Liberals believe that Affirmative Action must be retained to ensure that minorities are not discriminated against (Lakoff, 2010, pg. 225).   This to the Conservative increases regulation and costs on business and promotes reverse discrimination on the majority of citizens.

When it comes to privacy Liberals believe in this right as long as certain financial transactions are monitored and the abuse of children is not tolerated. Many Conservatives resist this and try to stop government funding for social programs that address child abuse such as programs that address spankings and other disciplinary action (Haidt, 2013, pg. 348).

Another privacy concern is the use of the airwaves and the internet and other forms of media and communication. This is generally understood by both Liberals and Conservatives as public and not private and that government agencies in the name of safety and homeland security can monitor them to deter criminal and terrorist activities.

Liberals believe that Federal property such as National Forests and Parks should be shared among the people for enjoyment and recreation. These lands are reserves for the protection of plant life and wildlife and to ensure the welfare and safety of various forms of life with restricted wild game hunting. The government is to be the custodian of the land to ensure that it is not molested by greedy corporations which will desecrate the lands with mines, roads and oil pipelines.

Many Conservatives argue that these lands were their forefather's lands that were used for cattle grazing and hunting and that these lands have been taken away from them. They resist paying the $5 per month per head fee for using public lands to graze their cattle, much cheaper than raising cattle on their own land. These lands to the Liberals are not for exploitation of the wealthy and that these ranchers are freeloading on society with an entitlement attitude. Theodore Roosevelt once said that these lands should not be "sacrificed to the short sighted greed of a few" (Green, pg. 372).

Military and War

Liberals in general are not for the military as a world policeman and support a smaller military presence worldwide. The military is often seen as a Conservative's welfare program that provides millions of jobs while military contractors make millions off of the tax payer's dollars (Lakoff, 2010, pg. 193). The United States spends more money on the military than all other countries in the world combined; why not spend that money on education for the children and on healthcare for the poor and the elderly who need it. For the Liberal, cutting social programs to pay for military budgets while trying to keep taxes low is immoral and unethical; this hurts the poor, the elderly and educational programs that are so desperately needed (Haidt, 2013, pg. 445).

Liberals tend to be peaceful and are strongly against war and other police actions and have tried to pass legislation against going to war in many cases. When Liberals have voted to go to war it is normally under the attempt to prevent the destruction of a group of people such as the Kurds in northern Iraq. Many Liberals believe that much of the animosity in the world comes from America's military aggressiveness and occupation. The world in general loves America; it is the military presence on their sovereign land that enrages many which in many ways encourages terrorist action against America and the West.

Conservatives argue that much like Communism in the 20th Century, Islamic extremism will eventually infiltrate the western hemisphere and take away the religious and economic freedoms that we now so enjoy. We must make our military strong in order to suppress and eliminate this enemy. Liberals argue back that Vietnam, Cuba and China are still Communist today and that millions of lives were lost and the economy of these countries destroyed by war for naught. We should not be in the business of changing governments through war; society will eventually take care of its self.

Prayer in School

Liberals believe that prayer is a matter of one's private life rather than being performed in public institutions and biased toward a specific Judeo-Christian faith. Religion should not be imposed upon people in a public forum that may risk making someone feel uncomfortable or alienating them in any way. There must be a "wall of separation," that strictly separates religion and civil society as religion can entwine with government and eventually become oppressive to minorities (Kuru, pg. 71).

Most Liberals feel that not only must religious institutions be free of government control but that government must be free from religious control as well. The "establishment clause" in most Liberal interpretations was intended to "limit government" from the control of religion and religion from controlling government (Garry, pg. 97). It was in fact for this very reason that various religious groups such as the Pilgrims, the Moravians and the Amish and Mennonite Anabaptists fled their home lands years ago. This was not only for freedom of religion to freely express their faith but also for freedom from religious oppression in their countries from State run religion.

Today, Jews, Muslims, Hindus as well as non-religious Atheistic and Agnostic people are still subject to religious activities that infer the Christian faith when they go to public car races and football games. Here, even today, prayers are said in "Jesus Name" and court houses across the nation still have the Ten Commandments written out for all to see.

Racial Issues

Liberals tend be sensitive to minority race prejudice and disadvantage and feel that government assistance to regulate and protect minorities is important. It is especially up to the government to defend those who are destitute and weak economically because of past racial biases. It is evident that many Conservatives in the South still strongly believe in what they call "Natural Law." This teaching States that God separated the races intending on them not to mix and that God meant to keep it this way (Botham, pg. 134). In 1954 the Supreme Court overruled many Southern States rules and enforced the desegregation of schools in *Brown vs Board of Education* (Kuru, pg. 50).

In another progressive win in 1967, the Supreme Court in the *Loving vs Virginia* case declared interracial marriage laws unconstitutional against views of more than 70% of the nation at that time (Kommers, pg. 378). As of 1967, sixteen Southern Conservative States still had anti- interracial marriage laws in place (Botham, pg. 152). Today 23% of Conservatives vs 1% of Liberals disapprove of interracial marriage.

Many Liberals feel that discrimination still exists across the country and that Affirmative Action rules still need to be enforced. Although they would like to see equal benefits for all in the workplace an in education, it is Conservatives that want these policies overturned. They feel that these rules are reverse discrimination and that many minorities are simply free rides on a system paid for by the taxpayer.

Religion

Liberals tend to be tolerant and have respect for all religion, many being agnostic or atheist secularist. In turn they have a natural attraction to foreign people, cultures and customs as well as non-traditional religious faiths. According to Jonathan Haidt, political preferences are not necessarily determined by your race or ethnicity and religion. However there is a good chance you are Liberal if you are black, Jewish or non-Christian and Conservative if you are a white protestant Christian with northern European ancestry (Haidt, 2013, pg. 398). Though many children may at first reject their parents' religious and political beliefs, most eventually end up with the same religious beliefs and political philosophy that one's parents had.

Sex and Marriage

Liberals tend to respect sexual preference even if it is not part of their personal traditional religious values. Sex outside of marriage even with partners of the same sex, is not immoral in its self as long harm does not occur. Most Liberals address sexual issues from the nurturing parent perspective where "moral self-interest" plays an important role in one's life (Lakoff, 2010, pg. 129). Moral self-interest works by each person striving to maximize their own "well-being" and therefore overall "well-being" for the community is achieved. For Liberals, prevention of harm is the moral issue, not the obeying of rules, especially religiously based rules.

Being on the left, they often have a higher tolerance for various sexual lifestyles and feel that the Conservative way of life with principles rooted in family and religion constrains individualism and one's personal freedoms. Liberals in general support legislation for gay couples to have the same rights as married couples. They feel that they have a moral system, a higher principle based on empathy and the ethics of care (Lakoff, 2010, pg. 418).

This strong belief in one's personal freedom goes in direct conflict to Conservative efforts to limit contraception to teens and prevent healthcare coverage for contraception and abortion through social programs. In addition to providing free contraception and keeping abortion legal, Liberals also support embryonic stem cell research from aborted fetuses as a way to improve health in the future for those who suffer from various genetic illnesses and diseases such as cancer.

Social Reform

Social reform is a primary part of the Liberal focus with an effort to invest the people's tax dollars back into society in order to improve individuals economic and health status. These reforms stem from the "status revolution" of the early 20th century where salaried professionals became distressed by oppressive big business and a perceived threat on their personal economic status (Carlisle, pg. viii). Today Liberals press for tax dollars to go to education all the way from pre-K through college in order to help social status rather than to use this money to build more prisons.

The Left

Liberals argue that primary education through college must be more affordable; a good education makes young people more able to get and hold a job and in the long run reduces crime and the need for more prisons. Student finance reform is one of the issues called for which would lower interest rates on student loans that would make college more accessible and affordable for more lower income families.

In an effort to attract good workers, many large corporations provide employees with benefits such as family leave and sick leave. However, most small companies and businesses in the United States cannot afford to do so. For this reason many Liberals have called for nationally subsidized leave in such cases as many European countries now have. The Family and Medical Leave Act of 1993 under Bill Clinton made some headway on this drive but did not go as far as many Liberals wished (Wilson, pg. 253).

European countries such as Denmark, Finland, Iceland, Norway and Sweden have had family-friendly policies for a long time. Liberals contend that even though the expansion of costs for social programs have increased the tax burden in these countries to the highest tax rates in the world, that despite these high taxes, these Nordic countries are still the some of the richest countries in the world. These very countries such as Denmark claim to have the happiest people in the world despite having the highest taxes in the world.

Strangely enough the health costs per person in the United States are double that of Sweden and about a hundred times that of India according to the World Health Organization (WHO). Also according to the WHO, in the United States in 2011, 45 million people went uninsured while 25 million were under insured; almost every advanced nation has better health statistics than the United States. About two out of every five people in the U.S. also reported having trouble paying their medical bills.

Liberals emphasis that in most developed countries other than the United States, medical care is affordable even though people have to pay out of pocket in many cases. The inability to pay for healthcare in countries without universal healthcare intensifies poor health and poor health makes it harder to rise out of poverty. People without healthcare are more vulnerable to disease and the poor get more ill more often and die sooner than those who can afford healthcare. To the Liberal, healthcare should be a human right; that the government is responsible to ensure that the basic needs of the American citizens are met (Lakoff, 2010, pg. 179). Conservatives argue that healthcare is not a human right but is a privilege that should be covered through private enterprise.

Taxes

Liberals believe privatization is dangerous as it takes tax payer dollars and gives it to companies whose only motive is making money and are not regulated as government entities are. It is the government's responsibility to regulate the economy and prevent inequalities; government can balance income and wealth by redistribution through social reform. This social process is to be controlled through regulation such as the minimum wage laws and assist the poor with food stamps, Medicaid, Welfare in order to control poverty as well as providing prenatal aid to poor woman and their infants (Wilson, pg. 25).

Wealth □

Liberals tend to support the concept of "equal distribution of wealth." Modern Liberalism is primarily a rebellion against the privileges of wealth. After the world wars until the 1980's, economic growth and equality grew together as both rich and poor gained from economic prosperity. From the 1980's till the present, inequality in wealth has grown exponentially in what some call the "Great Divergence" (Wilson, pg. 379). Exit polls since the 1970's indicate that people with higher incomes, $100,000 or more, are more likely to vote Conservative and are Republican.

Today, redistribution of wealth with higher taxes on the wealthy and by provisioning of benefits for all equally, seems to be the Liberal consensus. Their view is that most people who are wealthy are Conservative because they want to defend the privileges of wealth which is purely self-interest. Government should help the poor not for charity but as an obligation (Wilson, pg. 122).

Red and Blue

Many Conservatives feel that wealth is obtained through discipline and hard work; Liberals seem to contend that wealth is provided to mankind through nature and is impartial to human activity and that everyone has equal claim to this wealth. Many Liberal feel that people are only poor because others have taken more than their fair share.

Variables

Statistics

Statistics

Although there are primary characteristics that distinguish Conservatives and Liberals, there are also clear subtypes within each group that add variation to people's social, religious, and political beliefs and expressions. These subtypes can be broken down and identified by race, age, gender, religion, wealth, level of education, geographic location, and whether those polled live in urban or rural areas. Additionally, in recent years, many people have become disenfranchised with party affiliation, avoiding being considered Republicans or Democrats and now embracing Independent status. Although they identify as Independent, many of them still tend to vote either Conservative or Liberal in Presidential elections.

The percentages provided in the following text may not necessarily add up to 100% as those who are Independent or non-committed make up the remainder. These numbers vary in local and state elections, U.S. Congressional elections, or Presidential elections. Typically, those who vote Democrat are considered more Liberal and those who vote Republican, more Conservative.

According to the Pew Research Center's exit polls as of 2014, 39% of the United States population identified themselves as Independents, 32% as Liberal

Democrats, and only 23% as Conservative Republicans. When left or right-leaning Independents are taken into account, 48% of the United States population identifies as Liberal while only 39% identify as Conservative. Regarding voter registration, 48% identify as Liberal and lean Democratic compared to 43% who identify as Conservative and lean Republican.

Race

Different ethnic groups tend to lean in different political directions:

African Americans: 11% Conservative, 80% Liberal.
Asians: 23% Conservative, 65% Liberal.
Hispanics: 26% Conservative, 56% Liberal.
Whites: 49% Conservative, 40% Liberal.

Within the white demographic:

American Irish: 48% Conservative, 51% Liberal (making up close to 10% of the population).
Italian Americans: 30% Conservative, 37% Liberal (the fifth largest ethnic community in the country).
Polish Americans: 26% Conservative, 37% Liberal.

Variables

Gender and Age

When considering gender:

Men - 54% identify as Conservatives, while 44% view themselves as Liberal.
Women - 36% of are Conservative, with 52% leaning Liberal.
Unmarried individuals:
57% of women and 51% of men lean Liberal.

Generational differences also influence political leanings:

Millennials (born between the 1980s and early 2000s): 51% Liberal, 35% Conservative.
Silent Generation (born in the 1920s to early 1940s): 53% Liberal, 47% Conservative.

Religion

Religious affiliation significantly impacts political orientation:

White Evangelical Protestants: 63% Conservative, 22% Liberal.
Black Protestants: 11% Conservative, 82% Liberal.
Catholics: 40% Conservative, 48% Liberal.
Jews: 31% Conservative, 61% Liberal.
Mormons: 49% Conservative, 12% Liberal.
People with no religious affiliation: 61% Liberal, 25% Conservative.

Education

Higher education levels correlate with a greater likelihood of identifying as Liberal:

College degree or more: 52% Liberal, 40% Conservative.

White men without a higher education: 33% Liberal.

People without a college education: 57% Conservative.

Among those with advanced degrees:

Graduate school or PhD: 56% Liberal, 36% Conservative.

Observations

Recent studies indicate a substantial difference in cognitive processing between Liberals and Conservatives, suggesting a biological connection to political affiliation. In these studies, neuroimaging revealed that Conservative decision-making processes involve stimuli in the brain's right hemisphere, while Liberals show activity in the left hemisphere.

Conservatives tend to have larger amygdalae in the right temporal lobe, associated with "harm avoidance" (Absher, p. 100). The amygdala's primary role is in processing memory, decision-making, and emotional reactions. Additionally, Conservatives exhibit greater volume in the left insula and right entorhinal cortex. This aligns with other studies showing that

Conservatives have stronger repulsive responses to disgusting images, such as a person eating worms, compared to Liberals (Absher, p. 365).

Other research supports these findings, showing that Conservatives are more sensitive to threats and more easily startled by loud noises, exhibiting a greater "harm avoidance" reaction. This heightened sensitivity may explain why Conservatives are more protective of family, resistant to weapon regulations, more nationalistic, supportive of military growth, and more concerned about national security. This is often referred to as the "Conservative attitude syndrome," characterized by a generalized susceptibility to experiencing threat or anxiety in the face of uncertainty. The stereotype of Conservatives preferring large SUVs and pickup trucks for their safety may stem from their natural tendency toward "harm avoidance" and a need for security.

On the other hand, the study found that Liberals tend to have greater volume in the left anterior cingulate cortex (ACC) (Absher, p. 365). The ACC is involved in rational cognitive functions, reward anticipation, decision-making, empathy, impulse control, and emotion. This enhanced cognitive and decision-making ability may explain why Liberals are more likely to attend college and pursue higher education, as well as their tendency to "rationalize" everything. The ACC is also associated with monitoring uncertainty and handling conflicting information as a mode of "error control" when things are not properly balanced or are different. This might explain why empathy is a prominent trait among Liberals, who are more concerned about "equality" and "fairness." It may also account for Liberals' preference for diverse, exotic, and novel experiences, such as foreign sports cars and sushi, while Conservatives stick to traditional things that are less shocking and more familiar (Hibbing, p. 93).

Personality Traits

Conservatives are often characterized by a personality trait called "Conscientiousness," which draws them to familiar, safe, and solid things. They tend to encourage self-discipline, respect, and loyalty. Conscientious individuals are more dependable, honest, and considerate in relationships, and they value obedience to authority and the law (Hibbing, p. 14). They are also highly disciplined, driven, and strive for accomplishment and excellence in job performance.

In contrast, the tendency to enjoy more exotic and novel things is linked to "Openness to experience," a prominent Liberal trait. This makes Liberals less defensive in the face of perceived threats or new situations. Liberals are drawn to novelty, variety, diversity, and new ideas, particularly in culture and travel. These are individual "freedoms of choice," and such people often push the envelope and are deeply involved with music and abstract art (Hibbing, p. 104).

Morality

Jonathan Haidt's research suggests that people generally act ethically or morally only because they might be watched and caught; they will do what they want if they think they can get away with it. The real question is what ethics and morality mean to Liberals and Conservatives. There is a saying that "evil is in the eye of the beholder," indicating that both groups see ethics, immorality, and what is right or wrong differently.

Conservatives often view the lifestyles of Liberals as having an "anything goes" morality, believing that everything should be permissible and that inclusion and diversity should be embraced, regardless of how wrong or degenerate it may seem. Liberals, on the other hand, often perceive Conservatives as lacking basic compassion, especially toward oppressed minorities, while seemingly enjoying the prosperity of the rich and the suffering of the helpless.

Regarding moral concerns, Liberals tend to focus on individual-oriented values like compassion, harm, equality, and fairness, often supporting social programs for those in need. Conservatives, however, are more group/ family/ nation-oriented, emphasizing personal responsibility, purity, loyalty, respect for traditions, and authority. They also strive to reduce taxation and regulations that they believe burden their families, the economy, and their businesses.

Liberals and Conservatives disagree morally not because of rational reasoning but because of a natural predisposition to have different emotional reflexive responses to what they consider right or wrong (Hibbing, p. 107). These instantaneous emotional responses are shaped by genetics, family, friends, and other social influences over their lives and cannot be quickly changed through reasoning or persuasion. As a result, no one is purely Liberal or Conservative; people vary on different positions depending on their life experiences. For instance, one might be very Liberal regarding individual freedoms yet very Conservative regarding economics and business.

Liberals, with an "Openness" personality trait, tend to be concerned with "harm and fairness" and are sensitive to constraints on individual expression and freedoms. Conservatives, with a high "Conscientiousness" trait, are more concerned with issues that violate group-oriented norms, rules, or regulations. These moral foundations are dispositions in people's personalities that guide their reactions to various situations and shape their political opinions (Hibbing, p. 107). Studies of identical twins suggest that as much as forty or even fifty percent of our political ideas may have a genetic basis (Hibbing).

Both Liberals and Conservatives believe in the importance of fairness, cruelty, and injustice in determining right and wrong. However, these concepts are more central to the Liberal moral foundations of Care and Fairness, where inclusiveness often takes precedence over traditional notions of right and wrong. Conservatives, on the other hand, emphasize Authority, Loyalty, and Sanctity as their primary moral foundations, which many Liberals reject or personally dislike (Haidt, 2013, p. 183). Conservatives consistently prefer leaders who adhere to their moral objectives, while Liberals prefer leaders who can compromise and are inclusive in their approach to morality.

Red and Blue

Rhetoric

Persuasion

Rhetoric is the art of persuasion—the ability to get people to listen by saying things that resonate with their desires and concerns. People want to hear solutions to their immediate problems; they seek ideas that seem wise and experienced, offering hope. To persuade effectively, a speaker must move their audience to act by using appealing arguments and determined emotional manipulation.

Politicians, both Liberal and Conservative, use emotional appeal and metaphor to persuade people towards their cause. They employ these tactics to sway listeners' opinions on issues, often through relatable stories and allegories or by amplifying and arousing strong emotions. This not only convinces people that their approach is the best but also involves criticizing and demonizing the opposition.

A long-standing problem with rhetoric is that it has often been used for deceit rather than as a tool for discovering truth. Like used car salesmen, politicians are gifted with rhetoric and can persuade people to believe them, even on topics they lack understanding or capability. Consequently, they are often seen as untrustworthy liars.

Rhetoric has been the foundation for religious and political expression for thousands of years. Many ask why some people are persuaded to be Liberal and others Conservative in their religious and political persuasions. We know that people gravitate toward ideas and opinions that align with their interests, needs, and wants. Conservative and Liberal ideologies, like most belief systems, are embraced because they satisfy different physiological and psychological needs.

Political Ideologies

What are these physiological and psychological needs, and where do political ideas and opinions come from? Why do certain individuals and groups gravitate toward Liberal or progressive beliefs, opinions, and values, while others lean toward Conservative or reactionary ones?

Some distinguish Liberalism as advocating for social change, while Conservatism resists social change and clings to traditions. Others see Liberalism as rejecting inequality, whereas Conservatism accepts or allows it. Another approach contrasts the progressive emphasis on individual change with the Conservative focus on family, nation, tradition, and conformity.

Understanding the underlying needs and motivations that drive political beliefs can shed light on why people adopt specific ideologies and how rhetoric can effectively influence these beliefs.

Hierarchy of Needs

Abraham Maslow, a well-known Jewish American psychologist, developed a concept known today as Maslow's Hierarchy of Needs. In 1943, he wrote a paper titled "*A Theory of Human Motivation*," where he explained his theory of Human Developmental Psychology. This theory is now represented as the pyramid of Maslow's Hierarchy of Needs.

The hierarchy begins with basic survival or physiological needs and progresses through safety needs, love and belonging, self-esteem, and finally self-actualization. This highest level, self-actualization, represents the desire for self-fulfillment where one can move beyond focusing on one's self and begin to focus on others.

Self-actualization is:

"The desire to become more and more what one is, to become everything that one is capable of becoming"

Maslow pg. 92

To rise to the next level in Maslow's hierarchy, one must first fulfill the lower needs as a prerequisite. Upon reaching self-actualization, an individual attains a sort of enlightenment, understanding that they have everything they need and can be at rest, without worry. From this place of fulfillment, one can now focus on others.

People throughout society are at different levels and have different needs. The poor must focus on their physiological needs, such as food and shelter. Others who have secured these basic necessities and live in middle-class society often focus on safety and health concerns, while others may have needs related to belonging and self-confidence.

Politicians often latch onto these needs and manipulate people by promising to address them. Liberals typically address the lower needs of shelter, food, and health, showing empathy for the poor to ensure these needs are met. Conservatives often focus on the safety needs of the middle class and wealthier individuals, and both groups address needs related to belonging and esteem. People lean left or right depending on where they stand concerning these needs. The reasons why individuals lean left or right and why they are Liberal or Conservative depend on several factors.

First, family plays a crucial role. Although many young people initially discard their parents' opinions during their teenage years, most tend to adopt similar persuasions as they grow older. Some scientists believe that up to 50% of whether one is Liberal or Conservative is determined by genetics, passed down from their parents. Although parents may lean Conservative or Liberal, society is almost evenly balanced at nearly 50/50, similar to the male and female population. Just as families have a relatively balanced male-to-female ratio, they also have a relatively balanced Conservative-to-Liberal ratio. This implies that the difference may be 50% genetically induced and 50% socially induced through relational influences.

Second, geography matters. People tend to adopt the prevailing beliefs of the area they grow up in, a process known as "Group Think." For example, individuals raised in the Southern United States are more likely to have Conservative views compared to those raised in the Northeast. If people do not align with the dominant views of their area, they often move to places where their beliefs are shared. For instance, a gay person growing up in a Conservative Southern area might move to a more gay-friendly city on the West Coast. Social networking is crucial for maintaining alliances and reputations, influencing individuals to blend in with like-minded people.

Big cities with diverse ethnic populations tend to produce more tolerant and Liberal individuals. Children in rural areas, with less ethnic diversity, often grow up protective of their heritage and faith, leaning more Conservative. City children, exposed to various races, cultures, and religions, naturally become more inclusive. In contrast, children from small towns with homogeneous populations may feel uncomfortable when exposed to diversity as adults.

Certain regions have traditional American families with roots tracing back to the nation's founding. These areas, predominantly Republican, Protestant, Conservative, and white, include the rural Southern and Midwestern States. A band around the center of the U.S. consists of German/Swiss Americans, including Amish and Mennonites, who are generally Conservative but hold Liberal views on issues like gay marriage and antiwar beliefs. The Northeast, influenced by Irish, Italian, and Jewish immigrants, tends to be more Liberal and inclusive. Western states like California and Oregon, with their history of international trade, are more ethnically and religiously diverse, leaning Liberal.

Despite the Red State and Blue State rhetoric, geography is not as significant in politics as it may seem. Most states are close to being 50/50, with only a small margin leaning left or right. The blend of urban and rural votes ensures that political divisions are always close and change from generation to generation.

Third, wealth is a factor. Republicans argue that the notion of the Republican Party being the "party of the rich" is a myth, citing that many of the richest congressional districts and counties vote Democrat. They point out that wealthy Liberal celebrities criticize Republicans as the "party of the rich" while benefiting from tax breaks and grants. Conservatives advocate for a free-market society with low taxes to strengthen the economy.

Liberals, on the other hand, claim that Conservative values like lower taxes and less regulation benefit wealthy business owners. Studies show that the wealthy are more likely to be Conservative and vote Republican. Wealthy individuals like Trump and the Koch brothers favor cutting government spending and social services, increasing inequality between the rich and poor.

Both sides accuse each other of being controlled by the wealthy. Income, however, is not as critical a factor as perceived but is an important rhetorical tool for both sides. In poorer Red States like Mississippi and Alabama, partisan views are sharply divided by income, while in wealthier Blue States; income has less impact on political views.

Political animosity today is higher than ever, with people resorting to name-calling. Almost nine out of ten Americans are dissatisfied with Washington, and divisions have increased significantly since the 1990s and early 2000s. Conservatives and Liberals now see each other as endangering the nation's welfare.

For Conservative business owners, economic stability and business survivability are key concerns. Socially concerned Liberals focus on increasing inequality and support social programs for the poor. Evidence shows rising animosity due to financial issues, with Liberals feeling that big money controls politics, undermining reforms for the average American.

Policies affecting ideologies include Social Security, minimum wage, and taxes (Gelman, pg. 21). While wealthy Hollywood and Arts industry individuals tend to be Liberal, there are more wealthy Conservative business owners. Large donations for Liberal causes come from unions and the media, while Conservative donations primarily come from wealthy individuals like the Koch brothers.

Fourth, education is a significant factor. Higher education levels correlate with a greater likelihood of identifying as Liberal, while those with only a high school education or less are more likely to identify as Conservative. Many Conservatives argue that colleges and universities have become Liberal "indoctrination centers" for feminists, vocal minority groups, anti-Wall Street groups, and the LGBTQ+ community.

Liberals, however, dispute this notion. Studies indicate that college does not make students significantly more Liberal. Although most professors lean Liberal and are often skeptical about religion, students' opinions do not change drastically between their freshman and senior years. While there is a slight shift to the left, this shift is also observed in similar age groups without higher education. Research suggests that college graduates tend to be more Liberal because students who choose to attend college are more Liberal initially.

Liberals believe that education will strengthen America economically by bringing back jobs that were outsourced to China, Southeast Asia, and Mexico. With lower-skilled jobs being offshored to other countries and computer systems and AI automating mundane tasks, the economy increasingly requires workers with higher education, skills, and talents best acquired through higher education. Therefore, making college affordable is a key vision for Liberals. Recently, the Biden-Harris Administration pushed for additional student loan debt relief in an effort to unburden millions of Americans grappling with educational debt.

Conservatives, however, argue that the lack of Conservative professors makes it challenging to present Conservative views accurately, leading to what they perceive as Liberal indoctrination. They point out that over 50% of college graduates are either unemployed or underemployed, attributing this to a Liberal education that does not provide practical training. With student loans becoming unaffordable, Conservatives advocate for prudent choices regarding higher education, emphasizing that there are viable alternatives to traditional four-year colleges and that most jobs do not require degrees.

The Mind and Decision-Making

According to John Absher in his book "Neuroimaging Personality," neuroimaging shows that Conservatives' decision-making processes activate the amygdalae, located in the brain's right temporal lobe, while Liberals' decision-making processes stimulate the left anterior cingulate cortex (ACC). This indicates that not only do these groups reason differently, but their reasoning often serves to justify pre-existing decisions rather than being the result of careful thought.

Research shows that higher education or higher IQ leads to generating more reasons to support one's arguments rather than understanding opposing viewpoints. Instead of rationally weighing evidence, most people act first and justify their actions later; wisdom from impartial evidence evaluation is rarely used. Moreover, people tend to follow those with the best arguments aligning with their feelings on issues.

To most people, moral standards are absolutes perceived as either right or wrong, with little room for middle ground. Even though people acknowledge diverse opinions on moral issues, they often believe that if they could fully explain their "facts" to others, those others would understand and change their views. This belief is especially strong in religious perspectives and is not much different from political thought.

In other words, most people have already made up their minds on issues like gay marriage and are unlikely to be swayed. Politicians, therefore, need to listen to learn what people want to hear, and then echo those sentiments to gain support. Especially older individuals are rarely swayed by new arguments; they listen and choose who they already agree with.

Manipulation and Rhetoric in Politics

Politics is not necessarily about manipulating those who disagree but about listening and learning in order to know what people want to hear. Most people do not take the time to think things through for themselves; they react based on existing feelings and thoughts unless forced to reconsider. Both Liberals and Conservatives primarily react rather than reason in politics and religion.

Rhetoric filled with critical and elaborate language attracts like-minded individuals. Among candidates with similar perspectives, the one with the strongest rhetorical skills will win over the people.

An example of Liberal rhetoric is Al Gore's statement at a 2004 Tennessee Democratic rally:

"(George Bush) betrayed this country! He played on our fears. He took America on an ill-conceived foreign adventure dangerous to our troops, an adventure preordained and planned before 9/11 ever took place!"

An example of Conservative rhetoric is Alan Keyes' remark during Barack Obama's 2004 U.S. Senate campaign:

"Christ would not vote for Barack Obama, because Barack Obama has voted to behave in a way that it is inconceivable for Christ to have behaved".

Rhetoric influences its audience's views without providing justifications for positions on issues. It aims to strengthen and elevate one's position while weakening or disparaging an opponent's, often using biased emotional language with powerful influence.

Rhetoric uses devices like praise, criticism, and excuses to try and alter the issues at hand in some way positively or negatively. This can strongly influence people to take a certain perspective on a subject or person without any form of reasoning or arguments.

Slanters are rhetorical triggers used to insert influence with a positive or negative slant on the listener's position on matters. Although they may seem deceptive, non-argumentative slanters do not necessarily mislead with the intent to promote falsehoods; there is nothing inherently wrong with persuasiveness.

Analogies compare one thing to another to make one appear better or worse. For example, Robin Williams once said, "Politicians are a lot like diapers; they should be changed frequently and for the same reason" (Farmer, Rick, pg. 1).

Euphemisms promote positive expressions in a speech. An example is replacing a negative word like "war" with a more positive term like "defense." For example, "I'm having a senior moment."

Down players are words or phrases used to make something seem insignificant or less worthy. Words like nevertheless, however, still, so-called, or merely often serve this purpose. For example, "John had a little bit of trouble in his calculus class but still will make a good math teacher."

Dysphemism's provide negative expressions. For example, replacing a common term like "freedom fighter" with "terrorist" or the word "pregnant" with "knocked up." Or, *The oil spill on the Gulf Coast is exterminating thousands of animals and wildlife.*

Emotive force refers to the feelings, attitudes, or emotions a word or expression conveys. Dr. King's "I Have a Dream" speech uses highly charged emotive language, such as referring to African Americans as "living on a lonely island of poverty in the midst of a vast ocean of material prosperity."

Gaffes are statements by politicians that are true but potentially damaging and should not have been said. In 2008, when talking with Joe the Plumber about small business owners and taxes, President Obama said, "I think when you spread the wealth around, it's good for everybody."

Hyperbole is exaggerated embellishment, such as "Everyone knows that" or President Roosevelt's statement, "The only thing we have to fear is fear itself."

Innuendos convey an opinion without personal commitment. For example, a gangster's remark, "Nice car you have here; it would be a real shame if something happened to it."

Loaded questions are based on unwarranted assumptions and require more than a yes or no answer. For example, "Who is to blame for this terrifying presidential campaign?"

Metaphors identify something as being similar to something else unrelated, for rhetorical effect. President Reagan used a metaphor when he said, "Why, this country is a shining city on a hill!"

Proof Surrogates suggest evidence without presenting it, such as "some people say." For example, *"According to the polls, most people approve of Clinton's decisions."*

Rhetorical definitions and stereotypes emotionally influence listeners, such as referring to abortion as "murdering the unborn" or assuming all Conservatives relate to NASCAR.

Ridicule and **sarcasm** are common rhetorical tools that help subtly persuade the listeners. For example, Donald Trump's tweet during the 2016 presidential campaign: *"The U.S. will invite El Chapo, the Mexican drug lord who just escaped prison, to become a U.S. citizen because our 'leaders' can't say no!"*

Passing assaults can appeal to those who see the speaker as aligned with their interests. For example, Trump's statement during the 2016 campaign: *"When Mexico sends its people, they're not sending their best... They're bringing drugs. They're bringing crime. They're rapists. And some, I assume, are good people."*

Plausible deniability allows politicians to deny knowledge of or responsibility for unacceptable acts. For example, Bill Clinton's plausible deniability regarding his affair until the stained dress was found.

Weaselers are vague, hedging words that allow for multiple interpretations. For example, "You can lose up to fifteen pounds a week."

Many great speakers who truly have valuable material, use **slanters** and other rhetorical tools to become more vivid and engaging. The difference between those who try to **deceive** and those who convey **wholesome information** is that the latter also provide reasons, arguments, and proof for their claims.

Hitler's Rhetorical Skills

Looking back into history, Hitler is often viewed as evil incarnate, notorious for his profane and boastful rhetoric. He was perhaps the greatest con-artist ever known, fully understanding the pivotal role of rhetoric in seizing power. After his failed coup d'état in 1924, he realized that his path to power lay through the ballot box. Without his extraordinary gift of persuasion, Hitler acknowledged he would never have attained such influence. He possessed a keen insight into human psychology, though he held contempt for the masses, remarking, "The broad masses are **blind and stupid** and don't know what they are doing. They are primitive in attitude; to convince people by **reasoned arguments** is always **impossible**" (Loebs, pg. 3).

Firstly, Hitler recognized that people are more **swayed** by **spoken words** than written ones; every major historical movement owes its strength to oratory, not to literature. To become a formidable force, he knew he had to master public speaking. By the age of thirty-two, Hitler had little public speaking experience, but by forty, he had become one of history's most persuasive speakers, albeit for malevolent purposes.

Secondly, propaganda played a critical role in Hitler's strategy. He understood that the **audience was the speech's objective** and that only the simplest and most straightforward ideas would resonate. Propaganda, whether based on facts, arguments, half-truths, rumors, or lies, aimed to shape public opinion. Hitler skillfully tailored his speeches to reflect **what the people wanted to hear**, rallying them with powerful assertions of Aryan racial superiority, portraying them as the ideal and pure race. He **animated** his language to effectively convey his ideas, recognizing propaganda as a potent tool, stating, *"Propaganda is a frightful weapon in the hand of an expert"* (Loebs, pg. 4).

Thirdly, Hitler believed in the power of **repetition** in propaganda. He insisted that propaganda must focus on a **few simple points**, reiterated consistently until ingrained in the public consciousness. He famously stated, *"The receptivity of the masses is very limited; their intelligence is small, but their power of forgetting is enormous. Consequently, all effective propaganda must **harp** on a few slogans until the last member of the public understands what you want him to understand by your slogan"* (Loebs, pg. 5). He emphasized that effective oration to sway crowds required **exaggeration** and **relentless repetition**.

Fourthly, **lies** were integral to Hitler's rhetorical strategy. He subscribed to the belief that the ends justified the means, making deception acceptable for the greater good of Germany. He declared:

*"For myself personally I would never tell a lie, but **there is no falsehood I would not perpetuate** for Germany's sake."*

He argued that while people might accept small lies, they would never suspect their leaders of bold falsehoods. He rationalized, "My task is to free men from the dirty and degrading ideas of conscience and morality" (Loebs, pg. 6).

Fifthly, Hitler's rhetoric was characterized by stark, **black-and-white** reasoning—right or wrong, truth or lie, with no room for ambiguity. He asserted, "The thinking of the people is not complicated but very simple and all of one piece. Their thinking does not have multiple shadings. It has positive and negative, love or hate, right or wrong, truth or lie but never half this way and half that way" (Marlin, pg. 81).

Sixthly, Hitler adhered to Cicero's Ciceronian Maxim, employing **melodious language, clarity, and powerful presentation** to evoke emotions rather than reasoned thought. He believed, *"Man is moved more by passion than by reason."* He viewed the majority of people as inherently emotional rather than rational, asserting, *"The people in their overwhelming majority are so feminine by nature and attitude that sober reasoning determines their thoughts and actions far* *less than emotions and feeling."* His intent was to **arouse**, **provoke**, and **incite** through his rhetoric (Loebs, pg. 6).

Aristotle aptly noted, "If it is urged that an abuse of the rhetorical faculty can work great mischief, the same charge can be brought against all good things even virtue itself, such as strength, health, wealth, and military skill. Rightly employed, they work the **greatest blessings**, and **wrongly employed** they work the utmost harm" (Loebs, pg. 7).

Modern Politics

Modern rhetoric in politics mirrors historical examples, with **Donald Trump** arguably standing out as one of the most adept politicians in recent years. Like all effective orators, Trump employs analogies, metaphors, ridicule, sarcasm, and passing assaults to cultivate a fervent following, particularly among those disillusioned with Washington's politics from both major parties. His rhetoric strategically employs slanters to sway opinions, framing issues with both positive and negative perspectives to resonate with his audience's concerns.

Trump's appeal lies in his **responsiveness to the audience**, energizing them with **emotive passion** and occasional **exaggeration**. His speeches remain straightforward, lacking extensive reasoning, yet emphasize **repeated slogans** to reinforce key points. He acknowledges the entrenched divisions, recognizing that while he won't sway Democrats, he solidifies support among his base by **promising what they desire**, even if achieving those goals seems implausible; things are black and white.

In contrast, politicians like John Kasich opt for a more positive approach, avoiding negative tactics. However, conservatives, who thrive on clear-cut distinctions of good versus bad, tend to favor combative rhetoric. They view political contests akin to sports matches—focusing on conflict rather than conciliation. Candidates who shun contentiousness often struggle, as audiences crave the intensity of a political brawl rather than amicable discourse.

Even among liberals, known for their inclusivity and less confrontational style, seasoned figures like Bernie Sanders and Hillary Clinton understand the necessity of aggressive rhetoric. They critique opponents and their policies vigorously to sway public opinion, employing colorful language to elevate themselves while undermining their rivals.

Those who speak authentically possess a unique charisma that transcends mere reasoning. Their clear delivery and instinctual understanding of their audience distinguish them as rhetorical experts. Ultimately, a politician's goal is to capture voters' minds and hearts through effective political rhetoric.

While politicians may seem deceptive in their attempts to influence public opinion, these non-argumentative slanters are not necessarily falsehoods. Winning elections is crucial, but retaining power through subsequent terms depends on delivering on promises made. Those exposed as true charlatans seldom receive a second chance, underscoring Aristotle's wisdom that, *"Rightly employed, [rhetorical skills] work the greatest blessings, and wrongly employed they work the utmost harm."*

Conclusion

Balance

Across America and globally, there appears to be a peculiar equilibrium between liberal and conservative viewpoints among people. Wherever you go, individuals from diverse racial, religious, and cultural backgrounds tend to split almost evenly, leaning either left or right in their political stances. Studies indicate that approximately 50% of this inclination is shaped by environmental influences such as geographical upbringing, religious affiliation, race, age, gender, and urban or rural environment.

For instance, a young non-religious black woman living in a city in the Northeast is likely to develop liberal leanings due to her daily environmental influences. Conversely, a middle-aged white Protestant man raised in the rural South or Midwest is inclined towards conservatism influenced by his surroundings.

The remaining 50% of political leaning is attributed to genetic factors, akin to the nearly equal global distribution between males and females. Research also suggests that conservative traits are metaphorically akin to a strict father figure—emphasizing self-discipline, respect for authority, and adherence to traditional values. In contrast, liberal traits align more with nurturing mother characteristics, advocating for social equality, and progressive policies.

Individuals rarely fit neatly into purely conservative or liberal categories; most people hold mixed views. For example, a conservative might oppose gun control while supporting environmental conservation and animal rights. Similarly, a liberal could advocate for government-funded healthcare, welfare, and education but not be in favor of abortion rights.

The Strict Father Model

George Lakoff's "Moral Politics" outlines contrasting political and social viewpoints through metaphorical family models. The conservative perspective, known as the "strict father" model, views the world as perilous and demanding. It promotes self-control, discipline, respect for authority, and the importance of rules and standards in life. Conservatives believe in the inherent human condition requiring individuals to strive for self-improvement through moral and ethical means, fostering personal and national prosperity.

Conservatives argue that social programs, which they view as government handouts, foster dependency rather than self-reliance. They advocate for minimal government intervention, arguing that excessive taxation hampers economic growth by redistributing wealth from the disciplined to the undisciplined. They emphasize the role of government in maintaining law and order through the criminal justice system, while promoting a free-market approach to business regulation.

Contemporary Conservative Agenda

Today's conservatives prioritize family values, national security, and upholding traditional religious customs. They oppose practices like abortion, physician-assisted suicide, euthanasia, and recreational drug use, believing these undermine societal morality and stability. Conservatives champion religious freedom while cautioning against non-traditional faiths.

They advocate for fair treatment but oppose policies like affirmative action and extensive human and animal rights protections, which they view as discriminatory and economically burdensome. Conservatives endorse strengthening law enforcement and military capabilities to combat crime and terrorism, advocating for stricter border controls and reduced regulations on business and energy sectors to stimulate economic growth.

Conservatives also criticize government spending on initiatives like public education and healthcare, advocating for privatization and reduced federal involvement. They argue for lower taxes, believing in individual responsibility and economic competition as drivers of prosperity. Privacy, for conservatives, may be sacrificed for national security in combating terrorist threats.

Evolution of Conservative Thought

Modern conservatism traces its roots to the post-Great Depression era reaction against Roosevelt's New Deal policies. By the late 1930s, "liberal" became synonymous with New Deal supporters, while post-

World War II, conservatives gained momentum through alliances between business interests and anti-union northern Democrats. Richard Nixon's presidency in 1968 further solidified conservative values amid the turmoil of the Vietnam War.

Under Ronald Reagan in the 1980s, conservatism thrived with tax cuts and military expansion to counter communism. Reagan epitomized conservative values with his emphasis on personal responsibility, strict justice, and a pro-death penalty stance. His administration marked a shift towards individualism and reduced government intervention, challenging the welfare-state ideals of the New Deal era.

Nurturing Mother: Liberal Perspectives

The "nurturing parent" model, or nurturing mother perspective in liberal politics, revolves around a morality rooted in familial values but approaches issues differently. Liberals view the world as fundamentally safe, believing in the inherent goodness of people, although they acknowledge existing challenges and dangers. They emphasize moral nurturance through empathy, understanding, and extending aid to those in need, advocating that self-care is crucial before one can effectively care for others. Parental roles are seen as nurturing and supportive, aiming to raise children who will in turn nurture others.

In governance and policy, liberals prioritize societal protections, such as welfare and social security nets. They advocate for governmental regulations to ensure fairness, competence, civil liberties, and equal treatment. Progressive values promote public service, fostering trust, accountability, and responsibility, aiming for an economy that benefits diverse groups across the nation. Cooperation over competition is valued, recognizing the importance of interdependence in society.

Modern Progressives

Modern or contemporary liberalism, also known as progressivism, emerged in response to social issues stemming from America's industrialization in the late 19th and early 20th centuries. It arose amid low wages, rising poverty, poor working conditions, and political corruption that exacerbated economic downturns. Progressives argued that legal freedoms alone, as provided by the Constitution and Bill of Rights, were insufficient for individuals to achieve their full potential.

These progressives critiqued what they saw as unchecked capitalism, leading to growing economic disparities and racial inequalities perpetuated by wealthy industrialists like Andrew Carnegie and John D. Rockefeller. This era saw the rise of labor unions advocating for workers' rights nationwide.

Today, liberals continue to champion civil liberties, advocating for the freedom to choose, including rights such as abortion, physician-assisted suicide, euthanasia, and recreational drug use. They support religious freedoms, including non-traditional practices and freedom from religious influence in public institutions, such as schools. Liberal achievements include abolishing public prayer in schools, seen as a step towards religious neutrality.

Equal treatment under the law is a cornerstone of progressive policy, supporting affirmative action, human rights, and animal rights. They advocate for economic equality through initiatives like minimum wage increases and equal pay for equal work, alongside immigration reform to assist the marginalized. Liberals endorse equal education opportunities through public schools and advocate for universal healthcare, exemplified by the Affordable Care Act.

Protection, for liberals, extends beyond military might or policing; it emphasizes environmental conservation, challenging big business and promoting renewable energy. They seek to abolish the death penalty, criticizing its racial bias, and advocate for criminal justice reforms to address systemic racism. Liberals promote stricter gun control measures to reduce crime and oppose discriminatory laws targeting racial and ethnic minorities and diverse sexual orientations. The legalization of same-sex marriage in Obergefell v. Hodges stands as a recent progressive milestone.

These approaches necessitate increased government involvement and expenditure, funded through higher taxes. Liberals reduce military spending believing resources should focus on domestic needs rather than global military expansion, which they view as corporate welfare. They argue that excessive military spending redirects funds from social programs and economic development.

Comparisons

Conservatives and liberals differ not only in their political philosophies but also in their cultural preferences and psychological traits. Conservatives tend to favor competitive activities like sports and prioritize efficiency in decision-making, often influenced by emotional responses. They typically favor American-made SUVs and parking by backing into spots. They enjoy NASCAR races, focusing on pragmatic solutions and value traditions and customs.

In contrast, liberals engage in intellectual pursuits such as philosophy, deliberating on issues with reasoned arguments. They prefer smaller, imported cars and drive straight into parking spots. Liberals appreciate events like the Tour de France, emphasizing innovation and openness to new ideas. They prioritize empathy and imagination, advocating for animal rights and environmental protection, and are more likely to embrace diverse lifestyles and alternative religious practices.

These differences underscore distinct political ideologies shaped by varying psychological profiles and cultural inclinations, illustrating the complex interplay between individual beliefs and societal values.

Idiots and Imbeciles

In every workplace and social setting, there are always those who label conservative politicians as idiots and liberal politicians as imbeciles. Liberals are criticized for supporting politicians who allocate tax money to causes perceived as undeserving, while conservatives are deemed foolish for backing leaders who prioritize big business and military spending.

However, the reality is quite different. These politicians have risen to high levels of responsibility through intelligence and strategy. To dismiss them as idiots would be simplistic and misguided. It's essential to evaluate our voting decisions based on **reasoned analysis** rather than succumbing to rhetorical appeals, slogans, and charismatic speeches that lack substance.

Age of Reason

Whether left or right, liberal or conservative, most people tend to listen to those who resonate with their own perspectives and values. Their speech and rhetoric are often shaped around these shared needs and beliefs. Many of these underlying values and needs are rooted in pre-existing biases formed during early years by one's environment. People, in general, do not base their philosophy of life and political affiliation solely on reason; rather, they are significantly influenced by their emotions and biases. These biases, often ingrained from a young age due to personal experiences and environmental factors, shape their worldview and guide their political and ideological leanings.

Conclusion

For instance, inner-city Black and Hispanic individuals may grow up perceiving white people as oppressive, wealthy landlords who appear indifferent to their struggles. Conversely, rural white individuals may view Black people as burdens on the system, living off their taxes and contributing to crime in their communities.

These perceptions are deeply influenced by personal experiences and societal narratives, leading to entrenched biases and divisions. Understanding these dynamics and resorting to **reason** is crucial for fostering dialogue and empathy across different communities whether or not one is liberal or conservative.

As Baruch Spinoza stated in "Ethics":

*"Men, in so far as they live in **obedience to reason** necessarily do only such things as are necessarily good for human nature, and consequently for each individual man."*

Block pg.171

By embracing reason, we can transcend our biases and work towards actions that benefit both individuals and society as a whole.

We Are Who We Are

It's crucial to recognize that everyone approaches problem-solving differently based on their genetic traits and upbringing. These factors influence whether one leans conservative or liberal on various issues. Personal traits like empathy, conscientiousness, and cognitive styles (left-brained vs. right-brained) also play significant roles. Geographical upbringing, race, religion, sexual orientation, and age further shape moral perspectives and priorities.

These diverse factors contribute to the richness of our societal fabric, fostering varied viewpoints and priorities without necessarily implying moral or ethical superiority.

We All Can Get Along!

Despite differences, fostering mutual understanding is essential. Acknowledging that some view issues like LGBTQ+ rights, climate change, and abortion through moral lenses is crucial for dialogue. People's moral priorities are shaped by personal experiences and beliefs, which can lead to diverse perspectives on complex issues.

Most individuals have good intentions but prioritize moral concerns differently. Finding common ground requires respectful dialogue and compromise, avoiding the pitfalls of extremist rhetoric that polarize society. **Reasoned** political deliberation and compromise, as exemplified by Rodney King's plea for unity, remain essential for forging equitable agreements that serve the broader public interest.

This approach encourages empathy, **reasoned debate**, and the recognition of shared humanity despite political differences.

Conclusion

"Why Can't We Be Friends" by WAR

Why can't we be friends
Why can't we be friends
Why can't we be friends
Why can't we be friends?

I seen you around for a long, long time, ya
I really remembered you when you drink my wine

Why can't we be friends
Why can't we be friends
Why can't we be friends
Why can't we be friends

I seen you walkin' down in Chinatown
I called you but you could not look around

Why can't we be friends
Why can't we be friends
Why can't we be friends
Why can't we be friends?

I bring my money to the welfare line
I see you standing in it every time

Why can't we be friends
Why can't we be friends
Why can't we be friends
Why can't we be friends?

Red and Blue

The color of your skin don't matter to me
As long as we can live in harmony

Why can't we be friends
Why can't we be friends
Why can't we be friends
Why can't we be friends?

I'd kinda like to be the President
So I can show you how your money's spent

Why can't we be friends
Why can't we be friends
Why can't we be friends
Why can't we be friends?

Sometimes I don't speak right
But yet I know what I'm talking about

Why can't we be friends
Why can't we be friends
Why can't we be friends
Why can't we be friends?

I know you're workin' for the CIA
They wouldn't have you in the Ma-fi-a

Why can't we be friends
Why can't we be friends
Why can't we be friends
Why can't we be friends? . .

References

Absher, John R (2016) Neuroimaging Personality, Social Cognition, and Character, Academic Press, London Wall, London UK

Alcorn, Randy (2009) Pro-Life Answers to Pro-Choice Arguments, Multnomah Books, Colorado Springs, CO, 80921

Baier, Lowell E. (2015) Inside the Equal Access to Justice Act: Environmental Litigation and the Crippling Battle over America's Lands, Endangered Species, and Critical Habitats, Rowman & Littlefield, Lanham Maryland, 20706

Bertram, Eva (1996) Drug War Politics: The Price of Denial, University of California Press, Berkley CA, 94720

Block (2009) Ethics and Teaching: A Religious Perspective on Revitalizing Education, , Springer Publishing Company, New York, NY 10036

Bolt, Paul J. (2005) American Defense Policy, Johns Hopkins University Press, Baltimore, Maryland 21218

Botham, Fay (2009) Almighty God Created the Races: Christianity, Interracial Marriage, and American Law, The University of North Carolina Press, Chapel Hill, NC 27514

Brown, Mary Beth (2011) The Faith of Ronald Reagan, Thomas Nelson Inc. , Nashville, TN 37214

Buckley, JR. , William F. (2011) American Conservative Thought in the Twentieth Century, Transaction Publishers, New Brunswick, NJ

Bush, Jeb (2014) Immigration Wars: Forging an American Solution, Simon and Schuster, New York, NY, 10020

Carlisle, Rodney P. (2005) Encyclopedia of Politics: The Left and the Right, SAGE Publications, Thousand Oaks CA, 91320

Chamberlain, Theodore J. (2000) Realized Religion: Relationship Between Religion & Health, Templeton Foundation Press, Radnor, PA, 19087

Cutler, David M. (2005) Your Money Or Your Life: Strong Medicine for America's Healthcare System, Oxford University Press, New York, NY, 10016

Dautrich, Kenneth (2015) The Enduring Democracy, Cengage Learning, Independence, KY 41051

Dennis, Mark (2010) Right, Wrong and Reality, CreateSpace Independent Publishing, On-Demand Publishing, LLC

Engs, Ruth Clifford (2001) Clean Living Movements: American Cycles of Health Reform, Praeger Publishers, Westport Ct, 06881

Farmer, Brian R. (2006) American Political Ideologies: An Introduction to the Major Systems of Thought in the 21st Century, McFarland & Company Publishers, Jefferson, North Carolina, 28640

References

Farmer, Rick (2007) Legislating Without Experience: Case Studies in State Legislative Term Limits, Lexington Books, Lanham, MD 20706

Forgas, Joseph P. (2015) Social Psychology and Politics, Psychology Press, Routledge, New York, NY, 10017

Garry, Patrick M. (2012) Limited Government and the Bill of Rights, University of Missouri Press, Columbia Missouri, 65201

Gelman, Andrew (2007) Quarterly Journal of Political Science, Rich State, Poor State, Red State, Blue State: What's the matter with Connecticut?

Goldstein, Leslie Friedman (1994) Contemporary Cases in Women's Rights, University of Wisconsin Press, Madison Wisconsin, 53717

Green, Michael S. (2015) Ideas and Movements that Shaped America: From the Bill of Rights to "Occupy Wall Street," ABC-CLIO, Santa Barbara CA, 93116

Haidt, Jonathan (2006) The Happiness Hypothesis: Finding Modern Truth in Ancient Wisdom, Basic Books, New York, NR, 10016

Haidt, Jonathan (2013) The Righteous Mind: Why Good People Are Divided by Politics and Religion, Random House, New York, NY, 10019

Harsanyi, David (2007) Nanny State: How Food Fascists, Tee totaling Do-Gooders, Priggish

Moralists, and other Boneheaded Bureaucrats are Turning America into a Nation of Children, Broadway Books, New York, NY 10019

Hayward, Steven (2009) The Age of Reagan: The Conservative Counterrevolution: 1980-1989, Random House Inc. , New York, NY

Hibbing, John R. (2013) Predisposed: Liberals, Conservatives, and the Biology of Political Differences, Routledge, New York, NY, 10017

IBP, Inc. (2015) United States Investment and Business Guide Volume 1 Strategic and Practical Information, International Business Publications, Washington D. C. 20003

Jurinski, James (2004) Religion on Trial: A Handbook with Cases, Laws, and Documents, ABC-CLIO, Santa Barbara CA, 93116

Keegan, Lynn (2010) End of Life: Nursing Solutions for Death with Dignity, Springer Publishing Company, New York, NY 10036

Kirk, Russell (2001) The Conservative Mind: From Burke to Eliot, Regnery Printing, Washington Dc. 20001

Kommers, Donald P. (2004) American Constitutional Law: Essays, Cases, and Comparative Notes, Rowman & Littlefield, Lanham, MD 20706

Kuru, Ahmet T. (2009) Secularism and State Policies Toward Religion: The United States, France, and

References

Turkey, Cambridge University Press, New York, NY, 10013

Lakoff, George (2010) Moral Politics: How Liberals and Conservatives Think, Second Edition, University of Chicago Press, Chicago, IL 60637

Lakoff, George (2014) The All New Don't Think of an Elephant: Know Your Values and Frame the Debate, Chelsea Green Publishing, White River junction, VT, 05001

Limbaugh, David (2007) Bankrupt: The Intellectual and Moral Bankruptcy of Today's Democratic Party Regnery Publishing, Washington DC, 20001

Lints, Richard (2013) Progressive and Conservative Religious Ideologies: The Tumultuous Decade of the 1960s, Ashgate Publishing, Ltd. , Burlington, VT 05401

Loebs, Bruce (2010) Hitler's Rhetorical Theory, Department of Communication & Rhetorical Studies Idaho State University

Margulies, Phillip (2006) The Department of Energy, This Is Your Government, Rosen Classroom, New York, NY, 10010

Marietta, Morgan (2012) A Citizen's Guide to American Ideology: Conservatism and Liberalism in Contemporary Politics, Routledge, New York, NY, 10017

Marlin, Randal (2002) Propaganda and the Ethics of Persuasion, Broadview Press, Orchard Park, New York, 14127

Maslow, Abraham (1954) Motivation and Personality, Harper and Row, New York, NY

Miroff, Bruce (2014) The Democratic Debate: American Politics in an Age of Change, Cengage Learning, Independence, KY 41051

Nathanson, Stephen (2001) An Eye for an Eye: The Immorality of Punishing by Death, Rowman & Littlefield, Lanham, Maryland 20706

Regan Tom (2004) The Case for Animal Rights, University of California Press, Berkley CA, 94720

Spitzer, Robert J. (2009) Gun Control: A Documentary and Reference Guide, Greenwood Publishing Group, Westport, CT, 06881

Steinzo, Rena (2008) Mother Earth and Uncle Sam: How Pollution and Hollow Government Hurt Our Kids, University of Texas Press, Austin TX 78713

Stone, Carolyn (2015) The Transformed School Counselor, Cengage Learning, Boston, MA 02210

Walsh, Anthony (2004) Race and Crime: A Biosocial Analysis, Nova Publishers, Hauppauge, New York, 11788

Wilson, Carter A. (2013) Public Policy: Continuity and Change, Second Edition Waveland Press, Long Grove Ill, 60047

References

Wilson John K.   (2009) Barack Obama: This Improbable Quest, Routledge, New York, NY, 10017

Zelizer, Julian E.   (2012) Governing America: The Revival of Political History, Princeton University Press, Princeton, NJ, 08540

Red and Blue

Index

Conclusion

137

Conclusion

143

Conclusion